Composing in the Classroom

RESOURCES OF MUSIC HANDBOOKS

General Editor: John Paynter

RESOURCES OF MUSIC HANDBOOKS

Composing in the Classroom

RUTH HARRIS AND ELIZABETH HAWKSLEY

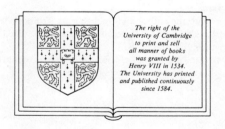

The right of the
University of Cambridge
to print and sell
all manner of books
was granted by
Henry VIII in 1534.
The University has printed
and published continuously
since 1584.

CAMBRIDGE UNIVERSITY PRESS

Cambridge

New York *Port Chester* *Melbourne* *Sydney*

Published by the Press Syndicate of the University of Cambridge
The Pitt Building, Trumpington Street, Cambridge CB2 1RP
40 West 20th Street, New York, NY 10011, USA
10 Stamford Road, Oakleigh, Melbourne 3166, Australia

© Cambridge University Press 1989

First published 1989

Printed in Great Britain at The Bath Press, Avon

British Library cataloguing in publication data
Harris, Ruth
  Composing in the classroom. – (Resources of music handbooks)
  1. Music. Composition
  I. Title II. Hawksley, Elizabeth
  III. Series
  781.6'1

ISBN 0 521 35104 9 hard cover
ISBN 0 521 35945 7 paperback

Publishers' acknowledgement
The Publishers would like to thank the author and publisher of 'Timothy Winters'
from *Collected Poems* by Charles Causley, published by Macmillan & Co. Ltd, for
permission to reproduce the words on pages 80–83.
  Every effort has been made to reach copyright holders; the Publishers would be glad
to hear from anyone whose rights they have unknowingly infringed.

PN

For Barry and Barry

II: *Contents*

II: *Foreword*

The GCSE has given us a music examination which, for the first time in the history of such things, requires every candidate to compose. The new emphasis upon practical and creative music-making must affect the way in which teachers plan the work for general music classes as well as for examination preparation.

Although there is no shortage of suggestions for improvisation and composition projects, as the authors of this book readily acknowledge, for teachers who have not previously worked in this way the mundane problems of organising such work in the classroom can be daunting; and that is an aspect which has been less thoroughly dealt with in the music education literature. Moreover, those who persevere discover that, in carrying through a composition course day by day, things do not necessarily become easier as time goes on. This is because, fundamentally, we are teaching from what is offered; that is to say, from what our pupils produce: not at all the same thing as imparting a received skill or an accepted body of knowledge. We have to be ready to comment purposefully upon unexpected turns of imagination, and to offer appropriate advice supported by the kind of classroom organisation that can foster many different kinds of progress – some of which will be very hard to predict.

Ruth Harris and Elizabeth Hawksley are both practising teachers who face these demands daily. The strength of their book lies not only in suggestions for suitable topics and starting-points but also in a very thorough analysis of the logistics of classroom management. They review with great care the things most likely to lead to success as well as the pitfalls we may encounter along the way; and I feel sure that, for any secondary school teacher planning a music course for the first three years that will also provide a good basis for music in the GCSE, this book will be an invaluable guide.

John Paynter

II: *About the authors*

Ruth Harris studied music and education at York University with Professor John Paynter. After professional training at Durham University she taught music at Manor Park Comprehensive School, Newcastle-upon-Tyne, then at Ferryhill Comprehensive School, County Durham, and was later appointed as teacher responsible for music at Willington Primary School in County Durham. During her teaching career she has taught music to all ages, from reception to A level.

Elizabeth Hawksley studied music at Bristol University and Goldsmiths College, London. After two years as a music teacher at Sidney Stringer School and Community College in Coventry, and four years at Hill Farm Junior School, Coventry, she became Head of Music at Hartshill Comprehensive School, Warwickshire, then moved to become Head of Music at Easington Comprehensive School in County Durham.

II: *Introduction*

This book is about composing as part of the music curriculum for 11- to 14-year-olds. Its main concern is with ways of overcoming the problems that teachers are likely to face when organising composing activities for classes of this age group.

Few music teachers today would disagree with the view that a school music course should be practically based and should include the opportunity for expressive work through composing. It is a view that has finally become established after many years and is embodied in both the HMI document, *Curriculum Matters 4: Music from 5 to 16* (HMSO), and the GCSE examination criteria.

Our feeling is that composing is central to the Lower School music course for two reasons: first for its worth in its own right, and secondly as a foundation course for potential GCSE candidates. We believe that teachers are now increasingly recognising the need to introduce composing as an activity in the lower secondary school so that all pupils have opportunities to work through the processes that composing involves. In the Lower School it is very much the introduction and development of the processes of composing that are important.

We have both had experience of trying to teach music under difficult conditions, with large classes, poor facilities, and the need to fight for realistic timetabling and sympathetic support; situations not conducive to practical work, let alone practical creative work. These experiences, coupled with a determination that all pupils *should* have the chance to compose, as they have the chance to write and to paint, have led us to try to find a way through seemingly incompatible pressures. This book is not meant to be the only answer; rather, we want to share ways we have found of tackling some of the problems.

The book is for all music teachers, newly qualified or experienced, to help the work they are doing. The practical organisational problems are common to most of us. In suggesting ways of dealing with these we have been deliberately detailed for the benefit of teachers who are new to the classroom, and some of the suggestions are included specifically for new teachers who are facing music classes for the first time, perhaps with no other specialist in the school. Before continuing, however, it is worth considering why our pupils should have the chance to compose.

If composing is to be part of our plan of work for our Lower School classes, we must be clear about the reasons for its having a place in the curriculum. Long before GCSE, many music teachers recognised composing as a worthwhile and essential activity. The GCSE criteria acknowledge composing alongside performing and listening as an integral part of the pupils' musical experience. The aims of music education as expressed in the HMI document *Music from 5 to 16* and as reflected in the GCSE programme, are a consistent plan for the whole of the pupils' school life. The early years of secondary school are an important part of this continuity and we must recognise that the kinds of experience being advocated are a relevant and central part of music education from 11 to 14.

As part of their education, pupils should have the chance to compose music. In doing this they are actively involved in discovering and exploring the elements of music which they then use to create their own composition. This requires them to unify sets of ideas and bring them to a satisfactory conclusion in their music. It is a process which calls upon their powers of reasoning and understanding, and which generates insight into their own ideas as well as those of others. The more varied the musical resources they have at their command to do this, the more scope they will have for developing their imaginative ideas.

The mastery of creative skills does not necessarily come about easily or spontaneously. There is sometimes the mistaken assumption that this area of learning simply allows the pupils a free run to do as they please in an unrestrained environment; but this is not the case.

The amount of critical aesthetic judgement that work of an experimental and exploratory nature constantly requires of the pupils is of such educational worth that it surely must be developed as part of their musical experience.

The idea of using the word 'composition' in relation to a piece of perhaps less than a minute in length, or 'performance' when initially all we may be listening to are a few notes played on a percussion instrument, appears at first too contrived to be taken seriously by some musicians. But as *teachers* of music we are concentrating on the processes involved, and early offerings are bound to be desperately simple compared with what we know to be possible at the height of musical attainment. We should think it very strange and unsatisfactory if, in their art and English lessons, pupils were never given the opportunity freely to express their own ideas or to use the tools of these disciplines in a personal way. We accept that however unskilled pupils are at drawing, we still call this activity 'drawing'. When they select and organise sounds into a piece of music, however simple and unskilled their attempts may be, they are still composing.

The development of performing and listening skills is an integral part of this process. From the earliest stages the pupils must be encouraged to play their compositions in the musical manner that performance requires. By insisting upon the proper conditions for performance we create the atmosphere in which pupils can enjoy performing seriously and will listen respectfully and critically to what is being played. It is important to establish this routine early on so that composing, performing and listening skills are developed together as playing becomes more sustained and the pieces more complicated.

The teacher's role is to help pupils to discover a variety of musical ideas and ways of playing that interest them, and we must be sensitive to the subjective nature of this process. We provide them with the resources to do this, but we also guide, nurture and help them to develop their own ideas.

There are particular and very special reasons why it can be difficult to plan a course for classes of this age group. These are to do with the age and abilities of the pupils, the problems of classroom organisation, the structuring of a composing course as part of a balanced curriculum and the teacher's conviction about the work. Perhaps for these reasons there has been a less common commitment to providing composing courses for these pupils. Before a sustained programme of work can be devised and made an integral part of the curriculum, teachers need to be convinced that it is feasible to teach music through composition.

It can be hard to find a starting-point with groups of pupils who may have had very different kinds of musical experience in their primary schools and outside the school. Ideally the early exploratory work will have been part of their primary school course, and the pupils will have some understanding of concepts such as rhythm, timbre and melody, and will have had opportunities to experiment with sounds as well as playing prepared pieces. But we must be ready in the first year of secondary school to cater for those who may have missed out, for a variety of reasons, on this kind of work in their primary education.

The implication of this is that, in some cases, we must start our classes with the kind of work which appears to be more suitable for the primary years; that is, the work involving the initial exploration of sounds. There is no way that we can avoid this if we want to develop composing skills with our pupils in a systematic way. These exploratory activities are the first stage of a long-term process and as such cannot be ignored, despite their seeming simplicity. We need to find a way of introducing them which is challenging and interesting to 11-year-olds. The way that this stage of the work is approached is of particular importance because it will only be accepted and respected by the pupils if we ourselves are convincing. If we can find a way of beginning which is of as much value to those pupils with some experience as it is to those who have none, then we shall have the right starting-point for a secondary school course.

It is worth taking a moment to look at one aspect which may be the source of a number of problems: these are activities which can make a lot of noise! Pupils of this age are usually taught in large classes, but it only takes two people working in the same place for the sounds of one to interfere with the other. If we are expecting upwards of twenty pupils to work with sounds, we have got to recognise that the problems of interference as well as those of an apparently disordered classroom noise have to be overcome.

Other musical activities – for example, pupils playing or singing prepared pieces of music – avoid the issue of interference and are a slightly more palatable intrusion on colleagues nearby. These *re*-creative activities are an essential and enjoyable part of the pupils' musical education and have an important place in the music curriculum. Teachers often concentrate upon them because they are a good way of giving pupils practical experience in music within a structure which is more manageable with a class working together in one room. But as soon as we ask our pupils to make their own music, singly or in groups within the class, the kind of freedom that is necessary brings with it a number of organisational problems; and one of these is how to deal with the noise. (Twenty electronic keyboards with sets of headphones can only give us a break for so long.)

Generally, it is impossible to provide a space for every pupil or group of pupils. Given the handicap of the usual arrangement of one class in one room, we need to ask ourselves if the benefits of composing can still be achieved, at least to some degree. If the answer is yes, and we are convinced that the unique experiences that the pupils have are worth striving for, then we have to recognise that conditions are rarely perfect because of the contradiction between large classes and the individual's need for silence within which to work. However, if we are aware from the outset that there are difficulties, we have a good chance of reducing the tensions by being conscious of them when planning. We can avoid potential trouble spots by planning the use of the space, time and other resources that we have at our disposal; so that, as nearly as is possible, we provide the best environment within which pupils can work.

All this requires effort from the teacher. It is not an easy option, and we really need to be sure about the benefits before we invest a lot of extra time and energy in planning and organising our classes. We need to believe that it is worth *our* while, particularly if this is a completely new approach with this age group; this will surely only be the case if we believe it is of real worth and benefit to the pupils in the context of their whole music education.

This book is concerned with finding ways of organising the work with pupils *in spite of* the difficulties of lack of space, limited equipment, and large – possibly mixed-ability – classes. We suggest ways of planning a composition course, and we look at the problems of setting up group activities. First, though, we must consider what this style of work means for the teacher.

Ruth Harris and Elizabeth Hawksley

II: *Authors' acknowledgements*

The authors wish to thank the following people: Pamela Dawson for her many hours of typing; Don Baxter, Dr Stephen Coniam, Helen Courtney, Jim O'Boyle, Len Rowe and Paul Usher; the pupils of Easington and Ferryhill Comprehensive Schools, County Durham, who volunteered some of their thoughts on composing for this book; John Paynter for his constant encouragement and guidance; and Annie Cave and Katherine James for being so helpful and supportive.

CHAPTER ONE

‖: *The teacher*

‖: *Teacher confidence*

Before considering our role in the classroom we ought to take an honest look at our private attitude towards teaching through composing. Many of us, especially in recent years, have become well acquainted with creative approaches to music education, either through practical experience in initial training and in-service courses, or through personal reading and research. Few of us, though, will have had experience of the process of composing as a central feature of our own music lessons when we were 11 years old.

Our musical education and training will have made the greatest demands on our performing, listening and critical skills; and it is in these areas that we will have become most competent and will feel most comfortable in our teaching. For those of us who have had some experience of composing it is likely that it will have been an area that was introduced once these other skills had been established.

Many music teachers compose, but few have learned about music *through* composing. Therefore only some will be able, easily, to identify with the activities that 11-year-olds are being asked to experience. The fact that our pupils' experience may be apart from our own is a distinction that we should be conscious of in our teaching.

Our own ability to be creative, and the amount of interest we have in composing at this level, are things we must consider honestly if we are serious about this work. If we are not entirely committed to the educational and musical benefits of this process with this age group, then the satisfaction to us as musicians is likely to be more elusive than with other forms of practical work. The very fact that we are offering this activity to all pupils means we know that, in many cases, the compositions are likely to be very basic. It takes time for composing work to develop and inevitably this will be at the expense of some other musical activity. We really have to decide whether we have sufficient interest in developing our own creative and critical skills, so that we can bring composing into equal prominence with listening and performing.

Most music teachers rely on their particular strengths as musicians as a focus for their teaching, and are unlikely to expose themselves to a situation in which they feel ill-prepared and vulnerable; most particularly when, in these other areas, they feel very capable. However, a sense of vulnerability and a lack of confidence are quite natural when teaching through composing because we must stand back and allow pupils to develop their own work in an environment which may, to the outside, seem chaotic – and with the risk that it could all go terribly wrong. With composing in the classroom, especially with a large class, there are always going to be risks, but there are ways of minimising them and developing confidence. We must be properly organised on the practical side, be totally clear about our role in the activity and, having made the commitment to start, work at it.

II: *The teacher's role*

From the pupils' point of view there are broadly three different stages of the activity:

Stage 1 The initial idea or stimulus
Stage 2 The practical activity of composing music by experimenting with ideas
Stage 3 The drawing together of these ideas in the performance of the piece

As teachers we should be acutely aware of the fine balance between the pupils' need for freedom and their need for our intervention and control. If we can see *our* role more specifically in terms of stages during the activity – although this may seem rather contrived – it could help us to recognise the areas where we feel confident, as well as those where we are less sure about the kind of contribution required of us. Where we have outlined three stages for the pupils, for the teacher during the lesson we identify four:

Stage 1 An introduction in which we are providing or discussing the stimulus
Stage 2 The stage (once the pupils have begun work) during which we observe and listen
Stage 3 The point at which we intervene with individuals or groups to give extra help or to discuss ideas
Stage 4 The point of conclusion when the music is shared and enjoyed

II: *Stage 1   Introducing a topic*

There is no shortage of books offering ideas for composing. Here, we are more concerned with the way in which teachers can translate and adapt such ideas to suit their particular situations. When introducing the activity it is important to be clear about the practical aims of the work you have chosen in relation to the pupils and the resources you are working with. This is an obvious point, but knowing *your* pupils and *your* resources is vital. It may well be that, before introducing composing to a new class, you will want to spend some time on other activities in order to find out what kinds of musical experience they have had.

Take as much or as little of the composing activity as you feel you can accomplish. When you are planning the lesson, break the activity down into stages so that you can determine what should be happening at any point during the lesson. If you are taking material from a book, don't be put off if your work seems less sophisticated than the ideas on the page. Even within one class, pupils will come up with very different work; and only a few of them might be able to achieve everything that an author suggests. Knowing this shouldn't stop us using their ideas as well as our own. Knowledge of our classes is crucial when interpreting an outside stimulus for our own situation.

Very often the introduction of a topic will include some form of practical explanation on the teacher's part, which also requires the pupils to demonstrate some understanding of a particular concept which is specific to that topic, either through discussion or practical example. As long as you are clear about how individual activities will collectively relate to the larger topic, then it is possible to see how shorter and more manageable activities can be introduced. For example, if the larger topic is 'To compose a suite of pieces entitled *The Four Seasons*', start by considering basic musical contrasts which best express the pupils' perception of the differences. For first-year pupils particularly, explore the kinds of instrument they feel are best suited to each season. Is there an aspect of any of the seasons which calls for a strong rhythmic character? Do any of the seasons call for special tempi or dynamic considerations? Work through each of these ideas separately. Having broken it down like this, you might find that it takes one group a few lessons to work through their ideas for just one section of the whole topic. So, when choosing any idea as a stimulus, try to break down the kinds of musical requirement that this might make on the pupils, and present these systematically as component parts of the whole topic.

It is important to be clear about what we will be doing and saying in introducing a topic to a class. What points do we actually want to make? How do we want to demonstrate them? Where do we want the pupils to be and what do we want them to do at this stage?

II: *Stage 2   Observing*

Once the activity has been introduced and the pupils are working, we reach the two stages which perhaps make the greatest demands on our practical teaching skills. The first of these, stage 2, requires us to observe and listen to the pupils working. We must be as patient as possible and not intervene too soon unless it is obvious that an individual or group is stuck. During this period of observation, the length of which may vary from five minutes to a whole lesson, it is helpful to consider the features of the compositions (techniques or musical ideas and their development) that you will want to discuss with individuals or groups when you reach stage 3, which is the point of intervention. Bear in mind the following points in relation to the work during the second stage.

- o   Decide how far from the particular activity that you have in mind you are prepared to let the pupils go. Sometimes it will be important to control or re-direct their work if you want them to focus on specific aspects of composition such as structure, chord sequences or timbre. At other times it is appropriate to allow the pupils to pursue ideas that seem only loosely related to the original stimulus. Whichever is appropriate, you must be clear about your aims for the class so that your reactions can be decisive.

- o   By observing and listening to each piece of work, try to identify how the pupils are interpreting the ideas so that your contribution, when you do intervene, will be built on their responses to the task. Absorb this information without comment at this stage if the pupils are working quite happily. It is very common, especially with groups, for it to be not immediately obvious how their work is relating to the original stimulus. It will very often become clear if they are left to work through their ideas. As with the point above, you will need to decide how long you want to leave them before interrupting.

- o   Although during this stage you should not actively criticise or discuss the music with the pupils, as they must have time to work this through for themselves, it is very important that, when circulating among the pupils and listening to their work, you encourage them to take the time to experiment and to try out a *variety* of ideas. As this is the crucial part of the process the pupils must feel comfortable enough, at their own pace, to reject ideas which do not satisfy them.

‖: *Stage 3   Intervening*

At some stage during the activity it is appropriate or necessary to intervene. The style of intervention will depend upon a number of things relating to the pupils' progress with the work, and it will determine our own role.

○ Find out how far the pupils have progressed with their plan of work by hearing them play as well as by discussing with them how they see the work developing.
○ Discuss any weak points that the pupils have identified for themselves, along with any ideas they have for strengthening these weaknesses.
○ Discuss any weak points that *you* think are there in relation to the pupils' perception of their music as well as yours as listener.
○ Using the material they have as a starting point, try to suggest ways in which their ideas can be improved (if you or the pupils are not satisfied that their piece is working successfully).

There will be times when ideas don't work and the piece has to be abandoned. We must reassure the pupils, who will be conscious of a sense of failure, that this is sometimes a part of any creative process. It is important to try to offer some constructive help with the direction that they can take in the light of this failure. It may be possible to suggest ways of developing one or two of their ideas in a different direction. We mustn't forget that we are expecting pupils to produce personal work in open surroundings. For some this is a difficulty in itself, so we must be particularly supportive when a lot of effort has apparently resulted in failure.

‖: *Stage 4   Concluding the topic*

You will need to decide the point at which any activity is concluded. Ideally pupils should be allowed as long as it takes to complete their pieces. In terms of organisation this will sometimes not be possible, particularly if the whole class are working together in one room. In this circumstance you will probably find that you need fairly rigid controls in terms of playing and listening times.

Not all pupils work at the same pace. This can have quite serious implications if they are all working together in one room. We shall look at this problem in detail in Chapter 3. For the moment we will assume that we have reached the point of conclusion and look at the form that this stage of the activity might take.

II: *Performance*

The final part of the activity might take the form of a performance either to you, to the rest of the class, or on to a tape recorder. However you choose to organise this, it is valuable and enjoyable for the pupils to hear the work of the other groups or individuals. Early on, some pupils will prefer tape recording their work to performing it live, so this facility should always be available. However, one of the general aims of the activity is to encourage pupils to feel relaxed about performing, and so we would hope to be able to encourage this with those who lack confidence in the beginning. Our aim is to try to promote a secure and respectful environment within which the pupils will be happy to perform their work. With some classes this will be difficult so we have to build up to it carefully. We have to be sensitive about the typical inhibitions of this age group, whose attitudes towards self-expression might sometimes prevent them from wanting to perform in front of each other. We have found, though, that by introducing the idea of performing their own work from the beginning of the first year and expecting the class to listen receptively, these things become an integral part of music lessons with the result that many inhibitions are dispelled. If it is possible, in terms of space, to separate pupils, then it can sometimes be useful for them to perform to each other in smaller groups.

The way that you treat these final performances can vary. Sometimes it is best to make up a 'concert' of the class music purely to be enjoyed as a set of finished pieces. Alternatively, you may want to use live performances as a forum for class discussion or further playing, paying particular attention to certain aspects of each composition. Again, you can tape record all the pieces and play them back to the class. This is an interesting alternative way of listening, as well as being a good record for you of the class work. These performances provide an opportunity, in a very informal way, to sow the seeds of 'listening' as an independent activity. We can use some of the ideas from the pieces to highlight different musical characteristics; aspects of the music which the pupils will be able to pick up when listening to other music. This experience gives them something to listen for which they can understand from first-hand experience.

You need not feel that you must always contrive a link between one activity and the next; it is possible and necessary to leave some work as finished without its having obvious connections to the next piece of work. Over a period of time all the various and varied projects which may appear disjointed will, nevertheless, have the common aim of developing composing skills. Only after a while might you begin to see the pupils pulling together the threads of the various activities, showing that there is a relationship between them. At the end of any project, however, the music which has been composed stands as the final event.

Having examined the teacher's role during the activity, three points emerge which seem obvious but which cannot be overemphasised: *know your resources*, *know your work* and *know your pupils*.

‖: *Know your resources*

This is more than simply knowing the numbers and kinds of instrument in your classroom stock. You must be at ease playing any of them and know what each is capable of doing. Most of us would assume ourselves to be capable of playing classroom percussion instruments, guitars and keyboards, but it is well worth spending some time on your own with these instruments, exploring their potential. Make sure that you only give out instruments that are suitable for the work you have in mind. Don't be tempted to give out poor or unsuitable instruments to make up the numbers. Do insist that beaters are held correctly for playing percussion instruments. Hold the beater across the ridge of the forefinger using the thumb to balance it (as you would pass a pen to someone).

‖: *Know your work*

Once you really know the instruments you have to work with, before starting any lesson you must be absolutely clear about the work. It is obviously important to know your objectives for the lesson but it is equally important to have some idea about the possible ways that the lesson will unfold. Because events are unpredictable to some extent, from the point of view of organisation, and in order to keep control, you might find it helpful to have support activities prepared. These activities may or may not have any direct connection with composing. If your main piece of work is to do with, say, timbre, prepare a few workcards with some supplementary ideas to try; for example, stretch their vocabulary by asking for descriptive words for the various timbres of instruments pictured on a card. This is an important aspect of classroom organisation which we will look at in more detail in Chapters 2 and 3.

‖: *Know your pupils*

Finally, the effectiveness and success of your work will depend very much on how well you know your pupils. It is particularly important that the pupils feel that their work matters to you; and they are only going to feel this if you know them individually. Each situation will dictate the best way to do this. Sometimes it is possible to start creative work from the first lesson of the first term and to get to know the pupils through their work. With other classes it soon becomes apparent that this is not going to be possible, and it is better to wait until some kind of rapport has been established before embarking on this style of work. In order to plan lessons effectively, it is helpful to know what to expect of a particular group: who has musical experience; who is timid or shy, boisterous or noisy; which pupils like to work together; who finds it difficult to participate in experimental activities. There are numerous elements which must be taken into account when planning lessons. Most of these we recognise instinctively, but being conscious of individual and class differences is a part of lesson planning.

II: *Pilot lessons*

The following lesson plans are included here for a number of reasons. They have been devised as 'pilot' lessons for 11-year-olds soon after their arrival from primary school. These lessons are significant for the teacher. They aim

- ○   to show how the pupils cope with this style of working
- ○   to reveal which pupils are familiar with this style of work
- ○   to give an initial impression of the way individuals respond to the musical demands of creative work
- ○   to illustrate the three stages of the pupils' activity (see page 8)
- ○   to highlight organisational problems
- ○   to suggest a structure for lesson planning (the seemingly obvious detail of these plans is included as an attempt at specifying areas where there may be difficulty)
- ○   to provide a starting point for a course of work by introducing some basic elements of music
- ○   to illustrate the four stages of the teacher's role in the activity

In these pilot lessons the pupils will be working in pairs. Early on this is a useful way of working from both the teacher's and pupils' points of view. For all it is a starting point for sharing and developing ideas. Pupils feel less exposed and seem able to work with more of the confidence they will need when they come to develop their work individually and in groups.

In the first lesson the pupils are composing melodies. In the second they are exploring timbre.

Teachers should work through both pilot lessons but only part A *or* part B of the second lesson (depending upon resources).

PILOT LESSON 1 Melodies and drones

In this lesson we take a very popular idea: composing a simple melody over a drone accompaniment. We want to find out how well the pupils respond to a number of simple musical concepts by combining them in a short piece which the pupils will compose, working in pairs. This lesson will introduce

- rhythmic drones
- simple melody on a pentatonic scale
- the idea of musical structure: the pattern A B A
- contrasts of tempo, rhythm, melody and dynamic

The lesson is devised in such a way as to be suitable for a mixed-ability class. Pupils who have completed Section A (see work cards) can be introduced, individually, to the ideas of structure and contrast in Section B.

The classroom Try to arrange the room using as much space as you can, with the pupils as far away from one another as possible. In a small room they will feel more isolated if they are not directly facing one another.

Instruments Use keyboards and instruments capable of playing a pentatonic scale for the melody. Make sure the pupils know clearly which notes they must use for the pentatonic scale and which will match their drone, either by labelling the keyboards or by removing unnecessary notes from the tuned percussion instruments. Any suitable tuned instruments can be used for the drone. Particularly effective will be those capable of playing a perfect 5th. Make use of any string players you may have in the class, or tune guitars in 5ths. Two pupils can work very effectively on one keyboard if you have a shortage of instruments.

Other resources It can be very useful for both pupils and teacher if the pairs have a work card which clearly and simply sets out the stages of the activity demonstrated in your introduction. Sets of cards like the ones on pages 16 and 17, and those described in the timbre lesson that follows, are going to build up into a useful resource, so it is worth taking the trouble to make them.

The lesson

Introduction There are many ways of introducing the concepts of rhythmic pattern, pulse and tempo. The object of this part of the lesson is to get

Tunes in Time

Section A

♪ Decide who will play the drone and who will play the melody, and which you want to compose first.

♪ What sort of drone sound do you want – sustained and smooth, or with a rhythmic pattern?

♪ Try out pentatonic tunes and choose the one that you like best.

♪ What does your tune do: move in steps, leap around, or a bit of both? Is the rhythm of your tune smooth or bouncy, fast or slow?

♪ How well does your drone fit with the melody? Would it be better to make them up together?

Tunes in Time

Section B

♪ Your music is now going to change in some way so that it is different from Section A. How are you going to do this? You could:

- keep the rhythms and melodies the same but just change the speed;

- keep the same drone, and find a contrasting melody;

- keep the same melody and change the drone;

- remember that playing soft and loud gives contrast to the music;

- change the pulse pattern from 2 to 3.

♪ However you decide to change the music, play B straight after A to see if you like the effect of the contrasts.

♪ Practise the whole piece so that you can play it all the way through.

♪ When the piece is finished, try swapping parts.

the pupils to demonstrate an awareness of these things. You many need to work at aspects of rhythm which children, even at this age, often find difficult: for example, the awareness of the extremes of tempo (they tend to play everything at a moderate pace); and the ability to repeat a rhythmic pattern, maintaining a steady pulse. It's always surprising to find pupils who use their natural sense of rhythm when *responding* to music in movement, singing or playing along, yet who have difficulties when it comes to controlling a rhythm for themselves. In this project they are going to use rhythmic patterns as a drone accompaniment to a melody. Demonstrate the sound of a pentatonic scale, perhaps using some tunes the pupils know. Illustrate different melodic shapes, emphasising some simple devices such as scalic movement, repetition or sequence.

Particularly at this early stage emphasise the importance of following through the points on the work card. Go through Section A with the class.

Activity   The pupils can now move away in their pairs to begin work. It is worth considering, and noting before the lesson, where each pair will go so that they can move easily and quickly and start work straight away. How they are positioned, particularly if they are all staying in the one room, will have a big effect on how well they are able to work.

Introduce Section B of the work card to each pair separately as the pupils successfully complete Section A. It is better to do it this way as some pupils are only able to work from a limited amount of introductory material, and may only complete Section A. There is also flexibility in the *way* you introduce Section B to a particular pair according to their ability. Furthermore, by introducing this section individually, you are able to use the pupils' own work on Section A to illustrate the points.

Performing and listening   Get the class together when they have finished so that they can all see and hear each other clearly. The drone and the melody could be performed separately at the beginning of a demonstration. The rest of the class could learn and join in with either of these parts. Any pupils who have worked on Section B can perform their pieces so that the others can listen for contrasts in their music.

PILOT LESSON 2   Introducing timbre

This lesson introduces timbre. It will help the pupils understand

○   that instruments are capable of making a variety of sounds with different characteristics and qualities

○   that families of instruments can produce sounds which differ in character from the kinds of sound produced by other families (for example, wood sounds are different from metal sounds)

o   that the quality of a sound is directly related to and determined by the material from which the instrument is made as well as the way in which it is played

o   that, by exploring this collection of sounds, a rich variety of tone colours is available with which to compose

o   that, by combining these timbres in a discriminating and aesthetically pleasing way, they are discovering *texture*

PART A

The classroom   When setting up the classroom, bear in mind

o   that the class will need to sit as a group with the teacher at the beginning and end of the lesson

o   that the pupils must be able to move easily from the class group to their work areas

o   that, initially, the instruments should be set up away from the pupils in order to get their full attention when introducing the topic

Instruments

o   choose contrasting instruments with which to demonstrate.

o   provide instruments for the pupils' work areas according to the number in the class. Try to provide contrasting instruments for each pair.

Other resources   Provide a word card for each pair. Initially the words on this card will help the pupils think about different types of sound. The choice of words is important as they must not produce sound effects, i.e. musical imitations of other sounds. Because the words are abstract, and therefore might be quite difficult for the pupils to grasp in isolation, it will be helpful when demonstrating to give the pupils some examples, or ask them to think of situations with which they would associate these kinds of sound.

faint	gentle	light	strong	sharp	sonorous
harsh	heavy	dainty	mellow	dull	resonant

The lesson

Introduction   Start the lesson by introducing the idea of *contrasts*. Explain perhaps that one thing is capable of having a number of contrasting features. The same face or voice can express many different moods; and the quality of light can change the way in which we see things. In the same way, a single musical instrument is capable of making a variety of different single sounds depending upon the way it is played. Each of these sounds has a *timbre*. Demonstrate this on one or two instruments and ask a few of the pupils to find contrasting timbres on one of the instruments. Don't be afraid to start with the absolutely basic contrast of playing gently and then playing forcefully. The pupils will hear these sounds as loud and soft, but we want them to find more than this. Loud and soft in themselves can have different qualities. To emphasise these differences, use some of the words from their cards. Show that a delicate, quiet sound differs from a dull, quiet sound, and that a harsh, loud sound differs from a resonant, loud sound.

Activity With the pupils at their instruments, ask them to find a sound to match each word on the card. They can do this sharing an instrument or comparing sounds if they have an instrument each.

Judge carefully the appropriate amount of time for this activity, bearing in mind the need to be flexible during a lesson and the need to allow time to move on to the next stage. If you are working for single lesson periods we would expect this stage to end the first lesson and be the starting-point for the second. In a double period allow about twenty minutes for the final stage.

PART B

The classroom The classroom can be set up with the pupils in pairs.

Instruments One of each available kind of instrument will be needed for demonstration. Provide two contrasting instruments for each pair.

The lesson

Introduction Timbre is determined by the material from which an instrument is made as well as by the way it is played. Wood, metal, skin and string have traditionally been used to make musical instruments because of the resonant properties of these materials. Explain and demonstrate these with a variety of instruments, emphasising that a single instrument can make a number of different sounds depending upon the way it is played. Each of these sounds has a timbre and some instruments are capable of producing more than one timbre. For example, try listening to the different sounds produced when a xylophone or a cymbal is struck with (a) a wooden and (b) a felt-headed beater.

Activity Because of the initial difficulty at times with the distinction between timbre and dynamic, the first activity is to explore timbre within the dynamic range on these different instruments. Concentrating first on quiet sounds, ask the class to find as many different timbres as they can. Do the same with loud sounds, as this will help the pupils understand that loud and soft in themselves are not timbres. The pairs could move around, working on as many different instruments as is practicable.

The next stage reinforces the idea of contrast in timbre. The task is to construct a short piece of music which demonstrates the various timbres of the instruments. One way of explaining what is required is to suggest the idea of a conversation in which each voice is represented by a different timbre. Contrasts in timbre contribute a lot to the interest of music. The juxtaposition of different sounds in music is one important feature of composing. Try to encourage the pupils to juxtapose contrasting sounds in their music.

Performing and listening (A and B) When listening to the pupils perform, make sure that the contrasts they are demonstrating include timbre and not just dynamic or rhythm.

Try to make sure that the whole class has heard the various instruments being played, as they probably won't have had time to explore all of them for themselves. Examine the different ways that the pupils have chosen to structure their work.

II: *Analysing the pilot lessons*

Let us look at what the pilot lessons have shown about the pupils, and at the demands this work makes on the teacher. The two lessons between them should certainly have given teachers an initial impression of the way each class works, as well as giving an indication of the particular interests and attitudes of individuals, which to some extent will influence the subsequent composing work you plan for them. The planning of further work will also depend upon any organisational problems that may have been highlighted by this exercise. It may be helpful to identify the cause of any weak spots during the lesson and to decide whether they have to do with your practical organisation or with the level and nature of the work. Remember that these pilot lessons are intended as a gauge. You may decide that the class is well prepared for this sort and style of work, or equally they may have found it difficult to work in this way; and you may need to think about ways of preparing your class to work creatively which are an expansion of these kinds of lessons.

If you identify a weak spot as an organisational problem, be clear about whether this is to do with your own organisation of the lesson or stems from some factor beyond your control, such as the size of the class in relation to resources (instruments, space, time). If lack of space or resources is the problem then you will have to plan your future practical work around these limitations (see Chapter 4, Instruments and space) If the weak spots were in your organisation of the lesson, try to be conscious of which of the four stages you found difficult and which parts of the lesson plan you feel you would want to expand.

II: *Checklist*

Within the context of the four stages outlined earlier in this chapter – introducing a topic, observing, intervening, concluding the topic – and having been through the pilot lessons, think about the following questions within each stage.

Stage 1 *Introducing a topic*

o Were you happy about the way the class communicated their understanding of the work they were going to do?

o Were you happy about the amount of time you gave to this part of the lesson?

o Were you satisfied that, by your style of presentation, the class understood that you were demonstrating examples of ideas and not presenting a definitive method which they had to imitate?

o Were you satisfied with the way the class moved into practical activity, or does the organisation of this need rethinking for your situation?

Stage 2 *Observing*

o Were you able to judge the right amount of time to leave each pair of pupils to work?

o Did you give yourself enough time to get round and hear the whole class?

o Were you confident that the noise was justifiable in this working situation?

o Did you establish a clear signal with the class to stop the work if necessary?

o Were you satisfied that the working arrangement was the best possible for the pupils?

Stage 3 *Intervening*

o Were you satisfied with the individual help you were able to give the pupils in terms of suggesting and developing ideas sensitively but decisively and efficiently?

o Did you find that you were constantly having to re-present and re-explain the activity? If so, did the pupils simply lack the confidence to get on, or were they not sure of what they were supposed to be doing?

○ Within this context, were you finding that pupils were worried about getting the work 'wrong'? (This kind of information will help you in the way you present work in stage 1 in future lessons.)

○ Did you find that you were having to spend too much time with some pupils, thereby losing an oversight of the whole room?

○ If too much time was being spent with some pupils, would it have been helpful to have stopped the class and made some general points about the way the work was progressing? (This is also a useful device if you find that all pupils are working at a similar pace.)

○ Were you able to bring this section of the lesson to a close satisfactorily so that the pupils were ready to perform?

○ Did the pupils work at such different rates that you are going to need to provide supplementary activities for those who finish early, or were you satisfied that you are going to be able to suggest such work as the need arises?

Stage 4   Concluding the topic

○ Are you satisfied that you allowed enough time for this stage of the activity and that you made the most of each performance?

○ Was the class sufficiently prepared and settled for this part of the lesson for them to enjoy each other's performances?

○ How comfortable did you find the class as listeners to each other's work? Was there a lack of interest in each other's work; and if so, was this apathy, competitiveness, or self-centredness? All these are very natural responses in pupils of this age, but part of this stage is to stimulate interest in other people's ideas.

○ Had you anticipated a way of dealing with pupils who didn't want to perform, and were you clear about why they didn't want to? (You will need this information for subsequent occasions.)

Finally:

○ Did anything arise out of this work that you felt you wanted to develop or explore further in subsequent lessons? Does this give you a sense of how you see a course of work developing?

With this information about ourselves in mind, and with some idea about the aptitudes and abilities of the pupils, we need now to look in some detail at ways of planning a composing course for our Lower School classes.

II: *Planning a composing course*

In this chapter we look at ways in which the areas of the music curriculum can be balanced, and suggest ways of assessing early composing work. Proposals for the later third-year course are given in Chapter 5.

II: *Timetabling*

We must try to ensure that it is recognised within the school generally, that music makes particular demands on timetable planning. It is worth seeing how far improvements can be made in the timetabling of our subject. Although most of us are not directly involved in the overall school timetabling, we should ensure that the case for the needs of our course is put well in advance so that we can present a convincing argument for change where that is necessary. Many of us will be familiar with the types of problem that can be caused by inappropriate timetabling. A timetable should give us the size of class appropriate to practical work, in a suitable room for at least one continuous hour a week. If none of these demands is met then the teacher clearly has no support for this kind of work and will have very serious problems in trying to carry it out successfully. More likely, one or two but not all of our needs will be met by initial timetabling, and here we must make a stronger case for the future and try to work despite the difficulties. Many music teachers have to work in situations which are far from ideal; but where there are opportunities for improvement we must take them. Involving ourselves in timetabling is one such opportunity.

II: *The place of composing in the curriculum*

Success with composing depends to a large extent upon it having a significant place within the music curriculum. Composing is more likely to be effective and to produce convincing results if it is developed through a sustained programme of work. If it is included only as an occasional activity the pupils will not have the chance to develop their composing skills systematically; nor will it work as a vehicle for teaching them a lot about music.

Trying to produce a balanced curriculum which pays attention to all of the requirements of a good musical education, including the needs of creative work, can be a problem in itself. We must give proper consideration to the context of the work, and to the practical implications of organisation (for example, the time it takes to develop group work, classroom routine, etc.); otherwise the results are likely to be discouraging and questions will arise about the value of composing. There are numerous activities to co-ordinate when planning a music curriculum. The balance of these, in terms of course planning, will depend to a large extent upon the teacher's skills and priorities, the available facilities and the pupils' aptitudes.

There are various ways to plan the composing part of the course, of which the following are perhaps the most obvious.

o Devise a self-contained composing course within the music curriculum, the activities of which need not necessarily relate thematically to other areas of the music curriculum. Such a course would work on a modular basis throughout the year, blocks of, say, four to six weeks being devoted solely to composing.

o Design a composing course as part of an integrated music curriculum wherein all activities are linked by a theme.

o Make composing part of the school's overall creative/performing arts course, operating an integrated timetable for these subjects.

We are going to cover the first two. Teachers involved in an integrated timetable with other subjects will hopefully be able to apply some of these ideas to their particular circumstances.

II: *An independent composing course*

With this option a course of composing is devised as a separate feature of the music curriculum. The course concentrates on developing composing skills as well as those performing and listening skills that are an integral part of the composing activity. In structuring this course we need to devise a systematic method which will help the pupils to expand their natural talents for composing (which with many pupils of this age is largely an enthusiasm to experiment with sounds) and help them to develop new skills.

In planning the course it is necessary to bear in mind the aims which are practical within the allocated time. Simple pieces of composing work done properly can take a while, and pupils need to feel they have had time to do their work well, so it is better to be cautious than to over-estimate the amount of work that can be achieved. The course needs a structure which is methodical, in terms of these aims, but which doesn't stifle the essence of the activity: the pupils' creativity. Although it is important to devise a systematic method to give *ourselves* structure and direction, creativity makes demands in an unsystematic way; so be prepared for diversions which do not fit rigidly into your plan.

No one aspect of music exists in isolation, but as a teaching device it is useful to concentrate on some elements separately. This systematic unfolding will require flexibility, so that the highlighting of one particular element is an illuminating activity rather than a restrictive exercise. In this process, which is of course only one way of introducing composing, the pupils explore the elements of music so that they can hear the different characteristics and learn to make a more discriminating use of them in their music. Initially they compose small pieces which highlight and demonstrate their awareness of these individual parameters, so that we can be sure the pupils are conscious of the different qualities of these basic elements as tools for composing. The lessons which introduce these elements need to be supported by complementary lessons. This gives teachers the opportunity to devise their own supplementary material or use published material in a systematic way.

Criticisms

Commonly there are two criticisms of this approach: that the concepts of, say, *rhythm* or *timbre* are too abstract and intangible for pupils of this age to grasp and work with as musical ideas in themselves; and that the method of introducing the elements systematically is too restricting for genuine creative work. This whole area depends very much on the teacher's ability to stimulate an exciting atmosphere and to provide supporting ideas which are absorbing and interesting to the pupils. Then they will quickly see the relevance and point of the new information. There is a good argument for a long-term programme of work that concentrates on these elements individually. The extra detail gives the pupils a stronger resource with which to compose as they go along. But these exploratory stages take time and they must be planned carefully.

Planning courses

The charts on pages 28 and 29 are an outline of the way we have organised the first- and second-year courses with some classes in our own schools. The other activities, apart from composing, are included to show how we choose to balance the curriculum; but, of course, this is only one way of doing it.

We have, in this and the following schemes, defined the pupils' activities under five headings:

composing
playing skills
singing
performing
background and listening

We identify singing and playing skills as separate from the 'performing' category because this enables us to concentrate on a more specific structure for these aspects of the performing part of the course. It is important to remember that many pupils, when they arrive from primary school, need to develop playing skills before they can perform.

II: *Composing as part of an integrated music curriculum*

An alternative way of approaching the Lower School curriculum is to integrate all the activities. (This method is particularly suitable where resources for composing are limited.) The themes can be musical or non-musical. This is obviously only one possible way of co-ordinating activities with one possible set of themes. In the diagrams at the end of this chapter we suggest an outline of the activities that could be included in the plan of work for each of the six terms. It differs from the first approach in that all the activities of the curriculum, including the composing element, are co-ordinated under a series of themes.

In either of these schemes any aspects of composing will fit into the 'composing' parts of the syllabus, so long as they are chosen and introduced as part of the systematic plan of work.

We have not specified how or when to teach notation in either scheme. We expect this to present itself as a natural extension of some of the proposed activities, but as it will be determined by the abilities of the pupils in relation to the topics, it is impossible to say whether and when the need for it will arise. With some pupils it will not arise at all.

II: *Composing assignments*

At the end of each year we include a special composing assignment which concludes the pupils' composing work for the session. Each assignment is designed with two aims in mind. First, that it should be free and flexible enough to give the pupils ample opportunity to display their particular composing skills. Secondly, that it should give the teacher an opportunity to look in detail at each pupil's work and to assess his/her progress. We tend to set a more demanding task which can be attempted either in part or completely, depending upon the abilities of the pupils.

First-year course

Autumn Term

Composing 1
Pilot lessons

Rhythm and melody

Composing melodies
Shape, structure, rhythm
Sample lesson: Tuning in
Complementary lessons

Integral performing and listening skills
Controlling a rhythm
Learning to listen to each other
Starting to perform

Performing/Listening

Playing skills
Basic exploration of the keyboard, guitar, recorder, percussion, etc.

Singing
'Class band' – vocal and instrumental arrangements
Christmas repertoire

Background
Music related to the Christmas theme

Spring Term

Composing 2
Timbre

Exploring timbre
Properties of instruments, methods of playing, producing effect through timbre
Sample lesson: Tapestries
Complementary lessons

Integral performing and listening skills
Controlling the way an instrument is played
Discriminating between different instrumental sounds

Performing/Listening

Exploring instruments
Topic-based study on the instruments of jazz, folk, pop, classical, ethnic, electronic, avant-garde, band, etc.
Songs of different styles

Background
The origins of different styles of music

Summer Term

Performing/Listening

Playing skills
Ostinato
Rhythm patterns
Pentatonic scale including vocal and instrumental improvisation
Matching words to rhythms
Class ensemble work

Singing
With practised and improvised instrumental accompaniment

Composing 3
Words into music

Introducing song writing – words to melodies and rhythms

Special composing assignments
Writing a song or using a poem/story as a stimulus

Second-year course

	First half-term	Second half-term

Autumn Term

Performing/Listening

Developing playing skills
New guitar chords
Keyboard work

Chords
Triads, sequences, clusters

Rhythm
More complex patterns, e.g. tied notes, syncopation, cross rhythms

Classroom band
Arrangements and accompaniments

Performing/Listening

Words and music

Singing, playing and background

Practical project
Optional themes: film music, musicals, pop cantatas, blues, jazz, folk

Christmas repertoire
Optional activity – composing a Christmas song

Spring Term

Composing 4

Harmony and texture
Highlighting and developing harmony and texture in compositions
Complementary lessons

Integral performing and listening skills
Exchange of ideas between groups
Playing each other's compositions

Composing 5

Song writing and word setting

Some of these options
Unaccompanied vocal settings
Vocal setting with chordal accompaniment
Two-part pentatonic songs
Composing accompaniments to well-known songs
Composing a pop song

Integral performing and listening skills

Development of group performance

Summer Term

Performing/Listening

Background
Groups, bands, ensembles
The relationship and interaction of composers and performers of different styles of music,
e.g. jazz
ethnic
choral and orchestral
folk
brass and wind bands
pop

Composing 6

1 Special composing assignments

2 Free choice composing assignment
developing a previous piece of work
a new composition in an area of particular interest to the pupil

Tapestries

II: *Lesson plans*

The following lesson plans are examples of composing work for each of the first three terms of the course. They can be used in either scheme of work. Lessons suitable for the second year course are included in Chapters 3 and 4.

YEAR 1 TERM 1 Tuning in: Composing a melody

Some pupils will have had the experience of making up melodies and others will, in any case, find it a natural thing to do and be very good at it. Others will need more help. With all pupils at this stage we would want to extend their ability to compose a melody by exploring with them the various devices that are commonly used to produce a good tune. Ultimately the pupils have to find their melody for themselves, as no amount of technical planning and information will produce an inspired tune. But we can help them by doing two things: looking at simple devices, and giving them a starting-point if they need one. The amount of information we choose to give them will depend upon their abilities, which will become clearer after working through the pilot lessons (see Chapter 1).

We might start with the most obvious devices of repetition of a phrase and sequences, strong rhythm, and the contrast between stepwise movement and leaps. Rhythmic and tonal shape will help them to formulate melodic ideas, and the use of repetition and sequences can help them extend those ideas.

A few starting-points are set out as separate work cards for the pupils on pages 32 and 33. They will suit different ability levels.

YEAR 1 TERM 2 Introducing timbre: Tapestries

This lesson is designed to develop further an awareness of timbre, and introduces the concept of sounds being represented by symbols, in this case shapes and colours. It is also designed to help the pupils understand that an awareness of structure and texture can help them in their composition.

The personal and subjective nature of relating sound to colour makes it an enjoyable and interesting diversion for pupils of this age as a stimulus for composing. The patterns and shapes that they create in their designs will be re-interpreted in their music. This lesson explores the idea of finding sound to match colours, and movements to match shapes, which can be woven like the threads of a tapestry into a complete piece of fabric. This shows the pupils the relevance of a score as a symbolic representation either of what has been created or of what the composer expects to be played. It is a way of showing them that any system of notation is simply a set of instructions based on an agreed code from the composer to the performer which can include information

Work cards for Year 1 Term 1

A Find some notes to match this pattern. These could be the beginning of your tune.

Find some more notes to complete the tune and finish the pattern.

Try turning the card upside down to give you the beginning of a second tune. How is this tune different from the first one?

B Choose one of these rhythms as an accompaniment to your melody.

Repeat the one that you choose a few times as an introduction to your tune.

Remember that the rhythm of your *tune* doesn't have to be the same as your accompaniment.

C

Each tune is going to represent a person or an animal.

Think of a character each. What are they like? Would a tune for them be fast or slow? Would it move in steps or jump around? Would you play it quietly or loudly?

Find a tune for your character. Are your characters very different or quite similar?

Make up a short story which will include all your characters.

D

PENTATONIC TUNES

Use all black notes
or
C D E G A
or
D E F# A B   Find one of these sets of
or   notes on your instrument.
F G A C D
or
G A B D E

Make up a tune using one of these sets of notes.

Give your tune an interesting rhythm.

Tapestry 1

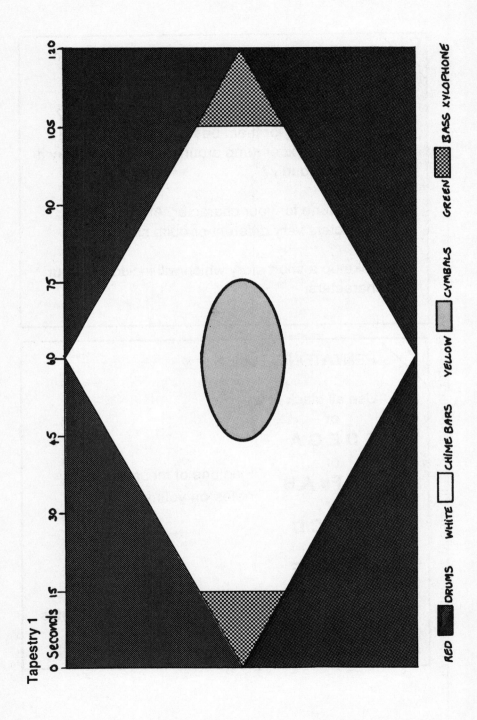

RED ▇ DRUMS   WHITE ☐ CHIME BARS   YELLOW ▨ CYMBALS   GREEN ▨ BASS XYLOPHONE

Example score: one possible interpretation of Tapestry 1

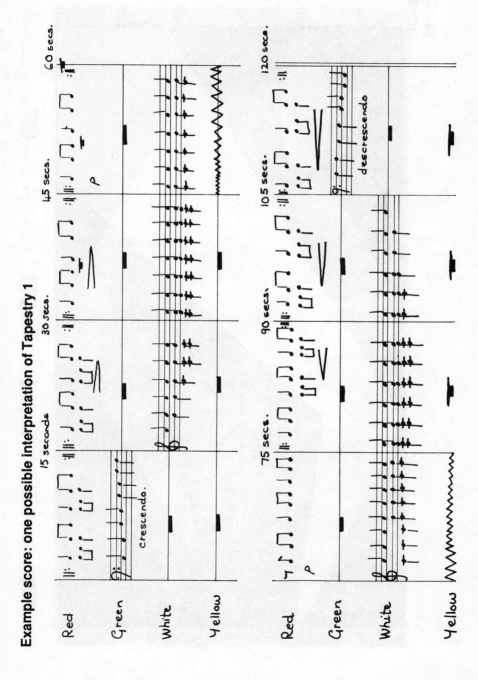

Tapestry 2

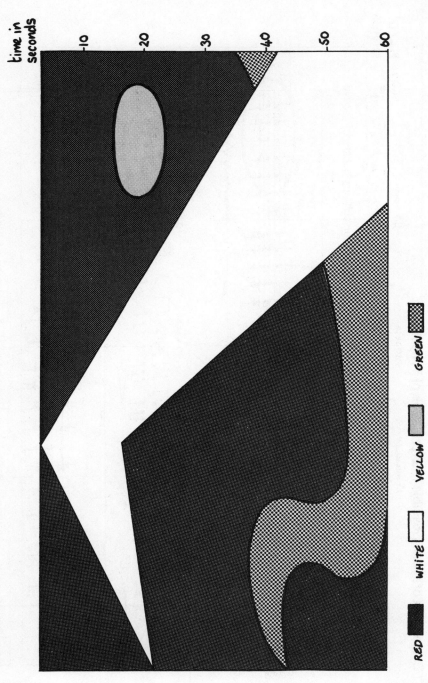

time in seconds

-10
-20
-30
-40
-50
-60

RED   WHITE   YELLOW   GREEN

Example score: one possible interpretation of Tapestry 2

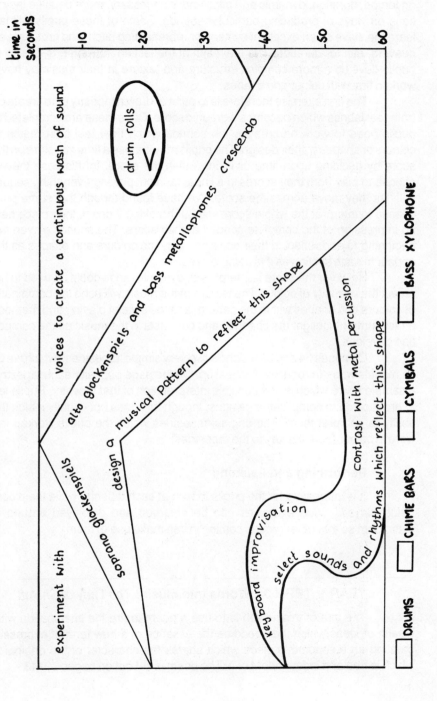

time in seconds

experiment with

voices to create a continuous wash of sound

soprano glockenspiels

alto glockenspiels and bass metallophones crescendo

design a musical pattern to reflect this shape

drum rolls

keyboard improvisation

select sounds and rhythms which reflect this shape

contrast with metal percussion

☐ DRUMS   ☐ CHIME BARS   ☐ CYMBALS   ☐ BASS XYLOPHONE

on tempo, duration, dynamic and pitch and, if necessary, more detailed instructions on ways of producing particular sounds. Some of these pupils will later learn the stave as an excellent system for representing pitch, and crotchets and quavers, etc. for duration. The main aim of the lesson, however, is to help the pupils develop a more complex structure and texture in their music by having worked first with colour and shapes.

The first exercise therefore is to paint or draw a tapestry or to create one from real fabrics which becomes a graphic score. Once these are completed the pupils need to work on creating the sounds which they feel best match the colours or shapes of their design. The pupils may impose a time structure on their score by deciding upon time divisions within the score. In this case they will choose to play from their scores in a linear fashion, playing everything sequentially as they move across the score. We have found though that some pupils choose to interpret the whole score without breaking it down, their piece being an impression of the complete content of their score. The sounds played from beginning to end reflect in their decisions only the colours and shapes as they appear in each section as it is being played.

However the score is interpreted, dynamic range could be used to help reflect the intensity of colour. The texture of the music will echo the combination of colours and shapes within the pattern, and the style of playing and method of attack further highlight the changes and contrasts in the music as the composition develops.

On pages 34 and 36 we show two very simple 'tapestries', which we use as models when introducing this lesson. On the page opposite each tapestry is a sample score which is one possible interpretation of that tapestry. Pupils tend to produce quite complicated designs, though this does not usually inhibit their ability to interpret them. The original tapestries which the pupils worked from were in colour (note the key to the tapestries).

Performing and listening

It is interesting for the pupils to look at each tapestry while the piece is being played. Good examples can be enlarged and displayed around the classroom so that other groups coming in can make use of them.

YEAR 1   TERM 3   Words into music: *The Lady of Shalott*

The aim of this lesson is to use a poem to fire the imagination with a wealth of ideas which then become the essence of a new form of expression, creating an autonomous piece which shares the character of the original but which is free and independent of it. The poem is set out on pages 39–43.

The Lady of Shalott

Part I

On either side the river lie
Long fields of barley and of rye,
That clothe the wold and meet the sky;　　　　**wold** *open, hilly*
And thro' the field the road runs by　　　　*countryside.*
　　To many-tower'd Camelot;　　　　　　5
And up and down the people go,
Gazing where the lilies blow　　　　　　**blow** *bloom.*
Round an island there below,
　　The island of Shalott.

Willows whiten, aspens quiver,　　　　10　　**aspen** *a tree whose leaves*
Little breezes dusk and shiver　　　　　　*tremble in a breeze.*
Thro' the wave that runs for ever
By the island in the river
　　Flowing down to Camelot.
Four gray walls, and four gray towers,　　15
Overlook a space of flowers,
And the silent isle imbowers　　　　　　**imbowers** *is home for.*
　　The Lady of Shalott.

By the margin, willow-veil'd,
Slide the heavy barges trail'd　　　　　　20
By slow horses; and unhail'd
The shallop flitteth silken-sail'd　　　　**shallop** *a light, open boat.*
　　Skimming down to Camelot:　　　　*flitteth glides swiftly.*
But who hath seen her wave her hand?
Or at the casement seen her stand?　　　25
Or is she known in all the land,
　　The Lady of Shalott?

Only reapers, reaping early　　　　　　**reapers** *corn gatherers.*
In among the bearded barley,
Hear a song that echoes cheerly　　　　30
From the river winding clearly,
　　Down to tower'd Camelot:
And by the moon the reaper weary,
Piling sheaves in uplands airy,
Listening, whispers ''Tis the fairy　　　35
　　Lady of Shalott.'

continued

Part II

There she weaves by night and day
A magic web with colours gay,
She has heard a whisper say,
A curse is on her if she stay   40
      To look down to Camelot.
She knows not what the curse may be,
And so she weaveth steadily,
And little other care hath she,
      The Lady of Shalott.   45

And moving thro' a mirror clear
That hangs before her all the year,
Shadows of the world appear.
There she sees the highway near
      Winding down to Camelot: 50
There the river eddy whirls,   *eddy small whirlpool.*
And there the surly village-churls,   *surly rough, sullen.*
And the red cloaks of market girls,   *churls working men.*
      Pass onward from Shalott.

Sometimes a troop of damsels glad,   55   *damsels young girls.*
An abbot on an ambling pad,   *ambling pad a horse,*
Sometimes a curly shepherd-lad,   *walking at a leisurely pace.*
Or long-haired page in crimson clad,
      Goes by to tower'd Camelot;
And sometimes thro' the mirror blue   60
The knights come riding two and two:
She hath no loyal knight and true,
      The Lady of Shalott.

But in her web she still delights
To weave the mirror's magic sights,   65
For often through the silent nights
A funeral, with plumes and lights,
      And music, went to Camelot:
Or when the moon was overhead,
Came two young lovers lately wed;   70
'I am half sick of shadows,' said
      The Lady of Shalott.

Part III

A bow-shot from her bower-eaves,
He rode between the barley-sheaves,
The sun came dazzling through the leaves,   75
And flamed upon the brazen greaves
        Of bold Sir Lancelot.
A red-cross knight for ever kneel'd
To a lady in his shield,
That sparkled on the yellow field,   80
        Beside remote Shalott.

The gemmy bridle glitter'd free,
Like to some branch of stars we see
Hung in the golden Galaxy.
The bridle bells rang merrily   85
        As he rode down to Camelot:
And from his blazon'd baldric slung
A mighty silver bugle hung,
And as he rode his armour rung,
        Beside remote Shalott.   90

All in the blue unclouded weather
Thick-jewell'd shone the saddle-leather,
The helmet and the helmet-feather
Burn'd like one burning flame together,
        As he rode down to Camelot.   95
As often thro' the purple night,
Below the starry clusters bright,
Some bearded meteor, trailing light,
        Moves over still Shalott.

His broad clear brow in sunlight glow'd;   100
On burnish'd hooves his war-horse trode;
From underneath his helmet flow'd
His coal-black curls as on he rode,
        As he rode down to Camelot.
From the bank and from the river   105
He flash'd into the crystal mirror,
'Tirra lirra,' by the river
        Sang Sir Lancelot.

bower-eaves the sloping roof of her bedroom.

brazen greaves brass-coloured armour.

gemmy jewelled.

blazon'd baldric a belt hanging from the shoulder, decorated with the knight's coat-of-arms.

burnish'd polished.

continued

She left the web, she left the loom,
She made three paces thro' the room,   *110*
She saw the water-lily bloom,
She saw the helmet and the plume,
    She look'd down to Camelot.
Out flew the web and floated wide;
The mirror crack'd from side to side;   *115*
'The curse is come upon me!' cried
    The Lady of Shalott.

Part IV

In the stormy east-wind straining,
The pale yellow woods were waning,
The broad stream in his banks complaining,   *120*
Heavily the low sky raining
    Over tower'd Camelot;
Down she came and found a boat
Beneath a willow left afloat,
And round about the prow she wrote   *125*
    The Lady of Shalott.

And down the river's dim expanse –
Like some bold seer in a trance,   **seer** *one who knows the*
Seeing all his own mischance –   *future.*
With a glassy countenance   *130*
    Did she look to Camelot.
And at the closing of the day
She loosed the chain, and down she lay;
The broad stream bore her far away,
    The Lady of Shalott.   *135*

Lying, robed in snowy white
That loosely flew to left and right –
The leaves upon her falling light –
Thro' the noises of the night
    She floated down to Camelot: *140*
And as the boat-head wound along
The willowy hills and fields among,
They heard her singing her last song,
    The Lady of Shalott.

Heard a carol, mournful, holy,   145   *mournful* full of sadness.
Chanted loudly, chanted lowly,
Till her blood was frozen slowly,
And her eyes were darken'd wholly,
    Turn'd to tower'd Camelot;
For ere she reached upon the tide   150
The first house by the water-side,
Singing in her song she died,
    The Lady of Shalott.

Under'tower and balcony,
By garden-wall and gallery,   155
A gleaming shape she floated by,
Dead-pale between the houses high,
    Silent into Camelot.
Out upon the wharfs they came,
Knight and burgher, lord and dame,   160   *burgher* citizen.
And round her prow they read her name,
    The Lady of Shalott.

Who is this? and what is here?
And in the lighted palace near
Died the sound of royal cheer;   165   *cheer* merrymaking.
And they cross'd themselves for fear,
    All the knights at Camelot:
But Lancelot mused a little space;
He said, 'She has a lovely face;
God in His mercy lend her grace,   170
    The Lady of Shalott.'

Tennyson's *The Lady of Shalott* is evocative of an era which appeals to pupils of this age group. The poem offers scope for related art/history/literature work, which is particularly helpful if music resources are limited and only a few people can compose their music at one time. We read and discuss the poem with the class and then together explore the musical possibilities. We invite suggestions about how, for example, melody, timbre, rhythm and other devices can be used to help compose a piece of music with the poem as its theme. After this the pupils can work in groups.

If we look at the poem in detail we see that there are numerous opportunities for creating a relationship between the written language and music. One approach for this particular poem is to concentrate on contrast, tone colour and structure as starting-points.

Contrast The most obvious contrast is the change of mood once the mirror cracks, at the end of Part III. The poem divides naturally into two unequal sections, and within these sections we have explored the different moods created by the characters, events and scenic descriptions. In the first section (up to the end of verse 13, line 117), further contrasts become apparent, most particularly between the solitude of the Lady in her tower and the activity on the river bank. The pupils chose a variety of musical devices to help them illustrate these contrasts. Many composed a sad, melodic theme for the Lady and a bright, full-textured piece for the people passing by. Few were able to resist a bold, rhythmic and usually very loud theme when they wanted to refer to Sir Lancelot.

Tone colour The poem stimulated a lot of thought about the use of instrumental colour. This was demonstrated in a number of ways, most notably by the pupils' choice of instruments for particular characters, and their selection of timbres to make up wholly impressionistic pieces which reflected the changing moods and atmospheres of the poem. Those pupils who opted to work on such impressionistic pieces used the strong colour imagery which runs through the poem as a basis for selecting tone colours. Generally the brightness of the first section contrasted well with the darker, more sombre colour images of the second. There are so many references to colour throughout the poem that the interpretation of these can be one starting-point that we suggest to pupils. Some pupils were so taken with the image of Sir Lancelot that they wanted to work on a piece just about him.

Structure With 11- to 12-year-old pupils we usually need to suggest some ideas for structuring their music. We have found that the following emerged as the most workable.

- o   If we choose to depict the reflected world in some way, verse 13 (lines 109–117) can become a central feature of the music's structure. Here the Lady of Shalott stops watching the world and the world starts to watch her, so the cracking mirror becomes a focal point in the structure of the music.
- o   Some of our groups chose to compose a suite of short episodes, each of which depicted some aspect of the story, for example people, the scenery, the mirror (this was represented by echoes in one piece), the flowing river, the Lady's death. One group used vocal effects by repeatedly chanting in a whisper, 'I am half sick of shadows' over an ever more impatient instrumental accompaniment culminating in a frenzy of metallic sounds as the glass shattered. Some groups created a piece which was a collection of images rather than sequences and others, more ambitiously, worked on sustaining themes for the Lady and Sir Lancelot, building other material around these.

This poem has worked very well as a stimulus for some of our classes but not for others. It is best to test the response of a class to a poem so that you can gauge their reaction and discuss the musical possibilities with them before deciding to use it.

II: *Assessment*

It is important for us as teachers to be able to assess our pupils and their work. Detailed information is increasingly required of us in the form of records of achievement of our pupils. We must be able to make clear, considered comments about their progress and have a means by which we can assess the work itself. These two factors form the basis of our assessment of the composing element of the course in the early years of secondary school. Knowing what to assess in a creative subject and how to assess it, particularly at this early stage, can be difficult. It might be helpful to break down our assessment into two categories: the composition, and the process of composing. There are no hard and fast rules for the assessment of this early work, but the following may be helpful as guidelines for teachers who find this a problem.

II: *Assessment of the composition*

Many of the criteria which are being used to assess GCSE compositions can be adapted, and in some cases modified, to suit the compositions of our Lower School pupils. Some pupils in their second year will be composing pieces which in their content, structure and musicality may well be beyond the aspirations of some fifth-form GCSE candidates. However, for the most part, we will be assessing pupils in the first two years who are beginning to develop their composing skills and whose work, therefore, will be less sophisticated than that of the fifth-form students. In particular, the less able and those who lack playing skills are often more capable of developing and expressing their imaginative ideas when working as part of a group. The interplay of ideas, and having more instruments to work with, provides the pupils with the opportunities to display such skills and ideas that they have within the context of a more complex piece. Groups of unskilled pupils especially seem to derive support from sharing their ideas in this way and are more willing to explore and experiment together. For many, group work will remain the best way for them to compose; and for this reason it is important for us to be clear about our response in terms of our assessment of the composition.

Second-year group work

The principal difference, therefore, between first year and fifth year, in terms of an assessment of the composition itself, is that, with Lower School pupils, we will most likely be assessing a *group* effort.

II: *Assessment of group composition*

We apply the criteria for assessment to a group composition in the same way that we would apply them to that of an individual's work. At this stage we are concerned only with the final piece and not with the particular contribution of any member of the group. This is because we want the pupils to see what set of absolute guidelines we use to assess a piece of music. We have found that a pupil can respond to this process more positively if she or he has to bear criticism of some aspects of her/his composition *as a member of a group*. When pupils begin to compose pieces on their own they will be more aware of our expectations of them and their music because of the process they have experienced as a member of a group.

If we examine the criteria for assessment for composing laid down by the Southern Examining Group in their syllabus for the 1988 GCSE Examination we shall see how these can be applied when assessing the less sophisticated composition in the Lower School. (We have chosen the Southern Examining Group as an example although the detail of the other Groups is very similar.)

II: *Criteria for assessment*

1 *The establishment and maintenance of style*

In terms of first-year compositions, 'style' is unlikely to mean a pastiche of any established musical styles. Rather, we are looking more at the ability of a group to establish or maintain a certain *character* in their music. This could mean being able to sustain a musical feature which we have suggested they should highlight in their music; or to sustain a mood or atmosphere which they feel is appropriate to the stimulus. We are also interested in the *cohesion*, as a group composition; so that, although it is produced by a number of pupils, the piece itself has unity and a consistent sense of direction.

2 *Development of material*

We can look at this in two ways. First, the pupils' use and development of the ideas they have explored with the teacher and with each other, and have then used in their composition; that is to say, how well or otherwise they have grouped and used particular compositional techniques that we have suggested they should explore. Secondly, how material has been developed internally within the piece. Has the group been able to develop ideas through repetition, for example? As an echo? By passing it between different instruments? By means of dynamic variance? Or at different pitches or speeds?

3 Understanding of instrument(s), voice(s) or other sound source(s) shown through effective use

This understanding will apply to the classroom percussion instruments that many first-year classes will be using as well as guitars, keyboards, and any other instrument they may have. How well, in relation to their playing skills, has the composition demonstrated their imaginative use of instruments? In what degree do we have the impression that a lack of playing skill has inhibited the expression of ideas? This is very important, as the quality of performance is entirely dependent upon the playing skills, but we must be sensitive, in assessment at this early stage, about good ideas which can only be poorly expressed. How well does the composition demonstrate their understanding of the expressive capabilities of the different instruments used?

4 Control of rhythmic, tonal, melodic, harmonic aspects through contrast and/or coherence

At this stage it is most likely that we will be looking at only one or two of these aspects in relation to the work that the pupils have done thus far in their course. In the first year, particularly, harmonic and tonal considerations might be incidental since the conscious use of tonality and harmony are aspects we would choose to concentrate on after the first year. However, it is important that the conscious and instinctive use of harmonic and tonal discrimination is acknowledged in assessment.

5 Control of texture, density, spacing through contrast and/or coherence

Group work is ideal for beginning to explore these aspects of composition. When assessing the group's composition, therefore, we need to know how they have combined instrumental and/or vocal sounds, and to what purpose? Is there an effective use of textural density and silence? How well has the group used these techniques to develop their material in the ways described in the second criterion?

6 Clear performance directions

There will be two kinds of comment which we can bear in mind when assessing the composition. The first is the pupils' explanation of how the performance of their piece might fall short of their ideal because of a lack of playing skill or available resources. Secondly – and we will get this from our observation of them working – how keen has the group been to demand an exactness in the way they choose their ideas to be played, for example, in terms of dynamic, tempo changes and control in expression?

7 Resourcefulness and originality

How determined has the group been to find and employ the resources which best suit their purposes? How well does the composition display originality in response to the stimulus? How have *un*original ideas been adapted in an original way? We would also want to acknowledge, in assessment, a composition which, at the end of a year's work, displays a *conscious* understanding of musical concepts explored during the course of the whole year.

8 Effectiveness and fluency of the composition as a whole

Generally pupils are responsive to each other's music – positively or negatively; they are a critical gauge which we cannot ignore when considering how effective a piece has been. A piece is effective if it meets with an enthusiastic response from the rest of the class, whether or not any of the above criteria have been fulfilled. Without fluency the music is likely to be less effective, as disjointed pieces more readily lose the attention of the listeners. Although its reception as a piece of music is important to us as a consideration of its effectiveness, we must be prepared to make musical judgements about the effectiveness of a piece which does not meet with immediate enthusiasm.

9 Powers of self-criticism used to obtain final version

This is one of the most important criteria for assessing first-year work, as much of our attitude towards the composition will be influenced by the process that we know the pupils have been through to achieve the final result. Our observations will have shown us the degrees of understanding and discrimination which the pupils demonstrate in their composing.

10   *Grasp of how the final version was evolved and the ability to explain/describe this*

This, and the previous criterion, together form the basis for the second set of criteria which we must employ in the assessment of Lower School work. These are criteria for the assessment of the *process* of composing in relation to individual pupils.

II: *Assessment of the process*

In assessing the development of composing skills we should be conscious of two aspects of the process. First, how well has the pupil developed and shown an understanding of *what it means to compose*? Secondly, how well is the pupil able to understand and apply the specific musical skills needed to compose?

1   *Understanding what it means to compose*

It is important to have some idea of pupils' attitudes to composing when examining their progress in dealing with composing skills. There will always be pupils who are difficult to motivate, and we have to make decisions about how far to pursue this activity with them.

In this area of assessment we need to consider the pupil's general reaction to the business of composing. How has the pupil responded in the following areas?

- o   Is there a willingness to explore and experiment with ideas?
- o   Is there an ability and readiness to assimilate new ideas?
- o   Is there an interest in making aesthetic judgements which involve the discriminating selection of ideas?
- o   Does the pupil persevere until a satisfying result is achieved?
- o   Is the pupil developing the confidence to use musical resources in a personal and expressive way to serve his or her own purpose?
- o   Is the pupil beginning to unify sets of ideas by planning a composition?
- o   Is he or she beginning to think about the music?

Our answers to these questions about individual pupils will help us in two ways. First, along with our general impression, they will help us to build up a picture of the pupil's response to composing from which we can comment on the development of specific musical skills. Secondly, these profiles, by ensuring that we are conscious of the attitudes and abilities of individual pupils, will collectively assist us in our own course evaluation.

2 Application of the skills needed to compose

In many cases this will be clearly related to playing skills, because at this early stage the groups' compositions are usually realised through practice. However, we must distinguish, as far as possible, *the idea* from *the ability to execute the idea* in performance. Some pupils will get round a lack of playing skill by directing others to perform; and some will be able to articulate the difference between their performance and the original idea, if this is necessary. The considerations we should have in mind for this part of the assessment are as follows:

○ What contribution has the pupil made to planning?
○ What contribution has the individual made to decisions about the varied use of resources?
○ Has the pupil displayed some powers of conjecture?
○ Has he or she developed understanding and application of the musical concepts which have been explored? (These might be rhythm, melody, timbre, texture, harmony, density, nuance, dynamic, form.)

II: *Effective monitoring*

Many music teachers in secondary schools will be teaching upwards of 300 different Lower School pupils every week. This makes detailed profile assessment of one aspect of the course a major commitment. We need to find an efficient way of recording information about a pupil's progress and abilities which is informative, in that it takes account of the criteria we have outlined. We need to be able to identify the specific areas of learning which we have outlined and then reconstitute them so that our assessment is an accurate reflection of each pupil's progress and abilities. How can we record information during the course of the year which will be useful when we come to make an assessment at the end of the year? We must be careful that any breakdown of the process that we choose to make does not throw up an inaccurate, incomplete or contrived picture of the pupil's development.

The criteria are useful only as an aid. They are areas to examine which can support our overall impression of the pupil's ability in creative work. Irrespective of the desirability of assessing the creative product, we must, as teachers, be able to assess our pupils' response to the demands of our teaching.

We include here two sample assessment sheets (see pages 52 and 53) which might be an aid to teachers in the assessment of composing

Assessment sheet 1

The process of composing

(Taped performance ☐)   Assessment of composition.......................

Name of pupil(s)...............................
Individual/group
composition...

Type of composition.........................   Title (if relevant)...

Musical features
Rhythmic control/interest
Melodic interest/development
Sensitive use of timbre/textural density
Use of dynamic
Display of harmonic/tonal awareness

General style and effectiveness
Sense of structure/unity
Maintenance of mood/character
Use of contrast/variety
Musical devices
Fluency

Originality
Imaginative use of musical ideas
Selection of voices/instruments
Any particularly unusual features

Performance directions
Musical detail
Method of playing
Is the performance inhibited by a lack of playing skills?
If so, specify. Can the pupil/group articulate this?

Assessment sheet 2

The development of composing skills

Name of pupil...................................... Year...

Period of observation...

Enthusiasm to explore and experiment with musical ideas

Assimilation of a given idea

Interpretation and application of a given musical idea

Involvement and interest in expressing ideas through music

Confidence in using musical resources and developing the necessary musical skills

Expansion of original musical ideas and powers of conjecture

Determination and perseverance in perfecting the piece

Demanding an exactness in the articulation and execution of ideas

Discrimination in selection and ability to reject ideas

work in the Lower School. They summarise the points made in this section of the chapter about (a) the process of composing in relation to the individual, and (b) the assessment of Lower School compositions.

II: *Course evaluation*

Finally, teachers responsible for the course evaluation might want to consider the following points.

1   General aims

Have the main aims of the course been fulfilled?

(a)   Have the pupils enjoyed and experienced music through composing?

(b)   Have the pupils developed their skills in composing?

(c)   Has the experience of composing expanded the pupils' understanding of music?

(d)   Have other educational and social aims been fulfilled?

2   Content

(a)   Was the course content suitable in terms of (i) age and ability (ii) appeal?

(b)   Did the course progress in a systematic way?

(c)   Were divergences followed up? Did these take over from the original plan in the case of any class?

(d)   Was adequate, relevant material always available for all needs?

(e)   Has account been taken of material which was (i) very successful (ii) a failure?

(f)   Was the composing content of the whole music course suitably balanced with other activities?

3   Method

(a)   Was the method of teaching appropriate to the needs of each class (i) for class work   (ii) for group work?

(b)   Were there times when the wrong approach was used? How did this become apparent and was the reason specific to that class?

(c)   Were you dissatisfied with any particular method or approach? Was this because of (i) poor preparation of content   (ii) poor organisation   (iii) lack of class motivation?

(d) Which methods or approaches were consistently successful, and can the reasons for their success be readily identified? Can the successful method be employed more widely?

(e) Has the presentation of the course been inhibited by lack of space or resources? If so, what are possible improvements?

4 Assessment and pupils' response

(a) Has the chosen method of assessment during the course been helpful in directing any changes in content, method or approach?

(b) Have pupils' responses, both positive and negative, been appropriately considered in terms of course content?

(c) Have the social and musical aims of group work been successfully achieved?

(d) Have pupils' verbal responses, as well as an assessment profile, contributed to the final evaluation?

5 Teacher's role

(a) Is there a suitable means of self-appraisal for the teacher during composing activities? Is this best agreed with colleagues?

(b) Can reasons be identified for any difficulty in teaching composing as against the demands of other aspects of the music course?

Generally, can the course be judged successful and worth continuing?

Having planned a course which is likely to involve pupils working together, it is important to consider the particular problems of organising group work for composing, and we examine these in detail in the next chapter.

YEAR 1 TERM 1

THEME
MELODIES

PLAYING SKILLS

Practice in and control of tuned and untuned percussion

Exploration of the workings of electronic keyboards

Fingerwork on keyboards

Easy guitar chords

BACKGROUND AND LISTENING

Focusing on melody

Famous popular melodies

Christmas music

SINGING

Songs which feature strong rhythmic patterns, particular structures and shapes in their melody

Christmas music

COMPOSING

Exploring melodic shape and structure in

○ tunes with rhythmic accompaniment

○ single and two-part pentatonic tunes

○ tunes in modes and major scales

PERFORMING

Arrangements of well-known melodies for classroom ensembles

Instrumental accompaniments to songs

YEAR 1 TERM 2

PLAYING SKILLS
Exploration of instrumental timbre

BACKGROUND AND LISTENING
Sounds from nature and from machines

The particular qualities of sound of solo instruments, live where possible

Different vocal styles

Effects produced by electronic instruments

THEME
SOUND SOURCES

SINGING
Songs from different sources
○ sea shanties
○ blues
○ folk songs

Experimental vocal work

COMPOSING
Pieces
○ which show ways of playing different instruments to produce different timbres
○ which highlight juxtaposed and combined timbres
○ which colour the texture of melodies and rhythms

PERFORMING
Arrangements which highlight families of instruments, e.g. drumming sequences

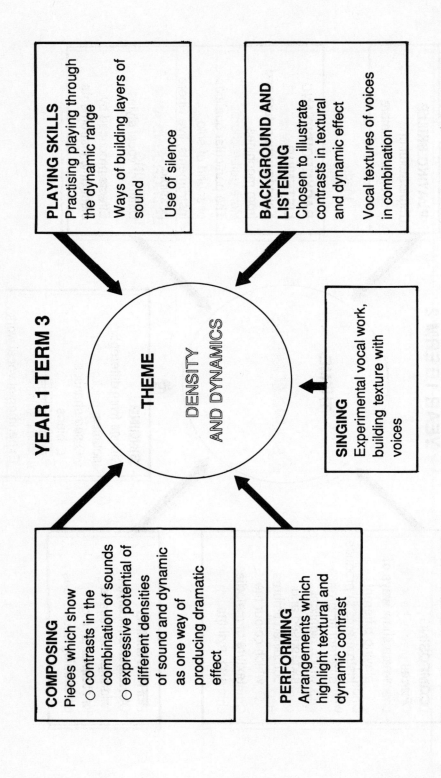

YEAR 1 TERM 3

THEME
DENSITY AND DYNAMICS

PLAYING SKILLS
Practising playing through the dynamic range

Ways of building layers of sound

Use of silence

BACKGROUND AND LISTENING
Chosen to illustrate contrasts in textural and dynamic effect

Vocal textures of voices in combination

SINGING
Experimental vocal work, building texture with voices

COMPOSING
Pieces which show
○ contrasts in the combination of sounds
○ expressive potential of different densities of sound and dynamic as one way of producing dramatic effect

PERFORMING
Arrangements which highlight textural and dynamic contrast

YEAR 2 TERM 1

THEME

CHORDS

PLAYING SKILLS

Chord building
- ○ pentatonic scale
- ○ major and minor triads
- ○ simple sequences
- ○ broken chords

Building clusters and exploring their effects

More guitar chords

BACKGROUND AND LISTENING

Examples of use of chords to illustrate practical work

SINGING

Simple two-part singing including background vocals

Songs for chordal accompaniment

COMPOSING

Chordal pieces based on chords and/or clusters

Chordal accompaniment to well-known tune

Melodic improvisation over chordal accompaniment

Composing a tune with chordal accompaniment

PERFORMING

Chordal accompaniment for songs on guitars, keyboards and tuned percussion

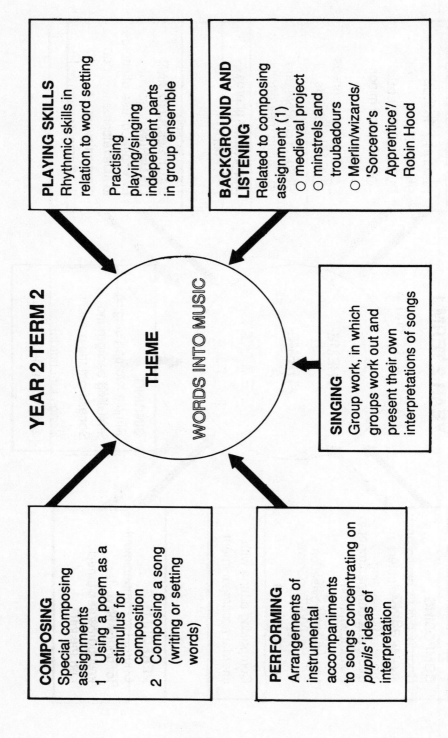

YEAR 2 TERM 2

THEME

WORDS INTO MUSIC

PLAYING SKILLS
Rhythmic skills in relation to word setting

Practising playing/singing independent parts in group ensemble

BACKGROUND AND LISTENING
Related to composing assignment (1)
○ medieval project
○ minstrels and troubadours
○ Merlin/wizards/ 'Sorceror's Apprentice'/ Robin Hood

SINGING
Group work, in which groups work out and present their own interpretations of songs

COMPOSING
Special composing assignments
1 Using a poem as a stimulus for composition
2 Composing a song (writing or setting words)

PERFORMING
Arrangements of instrumental accompaniments to songs concentrating on *pupils'* ideas of interpretation

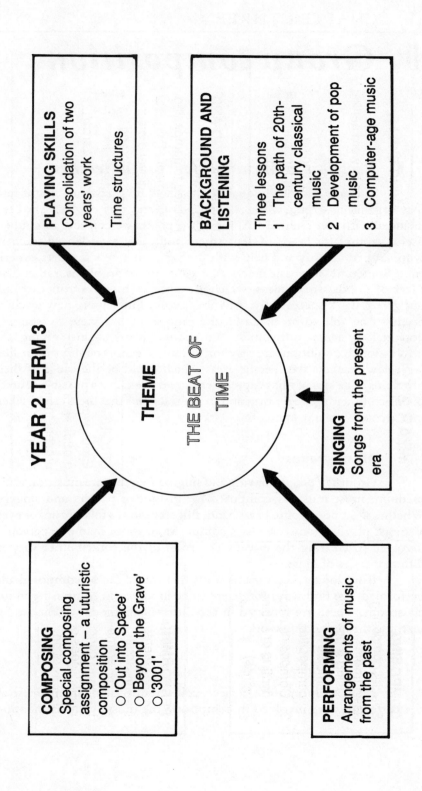

YEAR 2 TERM 3

THEME
THE BEAT OF TIME

PLAYING SKILLS
Consolidation of two years' work

Time structures

BACKGROUND AND LISTENING
Three lessons
1 The path of 20th-century classical music
2 Development of pop music
3 Computer-age music

SINGING
Songs from the present era

COMPOSING
Special composing assignment – a futuristic composition
○ 'Out into Space'
○ 'Beyond the Grave'
○ '3001'

PERFORMING
Arrangements of music from the past

CHAPTER THREE

II: *Group composition*

II: *Practical implications for student teachers*

Students and newly qualified teachers, in particular, might find that organising group work is a problem, and this chapter has been included with them in mind. Some of the points we consider might be a useful prompt for heads of department and other experienced teachers who have to identify and help with problems that new teachers experience. Sometimes it is basic practical, organisational problems, rather than a lack of enthusiasm or ideas, which prevent new teachers from carrying out group work successfully. Anyone involved in helping new teachers needs to be able to break down the process with a view to isolating potential or actual difficulties. We should guard against giving the impression that solutions are easy and instant. We must be able to consider with new teachers the specific areas which could be the cause of their problems. The aim of this chapter therefore is to examine possible sources of difficulty with group work, and to suggest ways that these can be taken into account when planning the work.

II: *Music groups*

Groups of people playing and singing together are music's natural medium; most music is composed for groups of players and singers. Whether it is a pop group, brass band, full orchestra, a folk group, or even a soloist playing someone else's composition, more than one person is involved in creating the music. The roles of the contributors vary in different styles of music.

If we look at the various ways that music can be composed and performed, we find ways for *groups* to be involved in composing in the classroom. These are reflected in the different methods we choose for teaching through group work.

Collective involvement

From the inception of a piece, collective decisions are made, so all the performers are involved in composing the music. This is the most likely way for the younger, less musically experienced pupils to become actively involved in composing. It is most probable at this early stage that the composition will evolve through playing and practice; through exchanging, experimenting with, rejecting and selecting ideas; and through the ultimate collective decision-making about how the piece will sound.

Players' interpretation

A composer provides the structure in the form of a musical idea (e.g. a melody or chord sequence) or perhaps a flexible graphic score, intending the performers to complete the composition through their interpretation. As in improvised music, in this situation in the classroom the musical ideas of one pupil, or our own starting-point, provide the basis for a composition. Other members of the group actively contribute to developing this. It is a useful way of working with mixed-ability classes where some of the less musically able pupils find it difficult to produce their own musical ideas, though it can be a method for helping them to do this. Once pupils start composing they sometimes come to their lessons with ideas for a piece, and getting a group to work with them gives them the chance to explore these in practice with others.

Individual composition

The selection and ordering of sounds to be played are decided by a single composer who may not be part of the performance. The composition is realised by performers who must interpret the composer's intentions. For most pupils of this age, composing in this way requires too strong a power of conjecture and sense of structure to be possible for them. It is possible though for some more musically able Lower School pupils to work in this way, and we must make sure that opportunities are provided for them to do so.

This is the method we most commonly associate with 'composing', especially when the music is to be notated, but we include in this category pupils who can compose their own music without notating it.

II: *Benefits*

Group work has many educational benefits as well as musical justifications. These are now widely recognised and group work is commonly used as a method of teaching in many other areas of the school

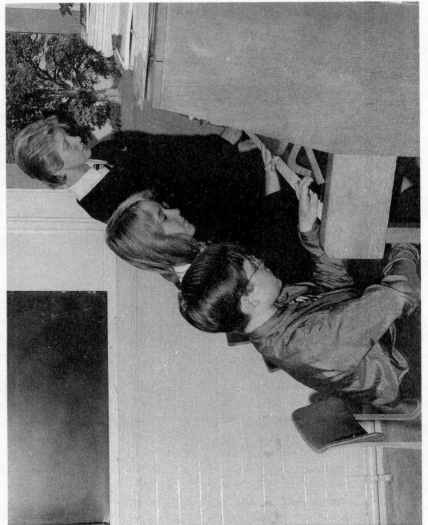

Composing with the piano

curriculum. As teachers we have a responsibility for giving pupils the kinds of experience that group work offers:

o   the development of confidence
o   the skills of corporate decision-making
o   the ability to defer to other people
o   respect for each other's work
o   learning constructive criticism
o   working freely within a disciplined environment
o   being responsible for and trusted with expensive equipment away from the teacher's immediate supervision.

These are all things which we have the opportunity to develop with our pupils through group work. As most pupils in the Lower School will be new to the activity of composing, and are likely therefore to be unskilled, the most productive way for them to compose is probably as part of a group.

II: *Noise*

As teachers we can take advantage of the social and educational benefits of group work. We are particularly fortunate as teachers *of music* that our subject lends itself so naturally to this style of working. Ironically, despite this, music is perhaps one of the hardest subjects to organise and control as a group activity because we encourage the groups to make a noise! So before beginning any group work in music, but especially composing, we must be certain that we have considered all angles of the activity so that we are in absolute control.

II: *Pupils' attitudes, aptitudes and characteristics*

As we mentioned in Chapter 2, knowing something about our pupils' aptitudes and individual characteristics is an important prerequisite for setting up group work. They contribute to the pupils' attitude to composing, an understanding of which will in turn affect our response in terms of work. There are always differences in character in any group of thirty or so people. This is no less true of a class in school. When organising an activity which demands such an individual response, we need to take account of these characteristics. We must recognise that however committed we are to the benefits of group work and to the whole principle of this style of teaching, we will occasionally come across a class with whom, because of a particular combination of characters within it, it is impossible to apply our desired method of working. It is best to identify such a class and consider them separately in terms of a plan of work. They may need a different approach, or it may not be possible to work in this way with them at all. It can be very debilitating when faced with such a class, but it is better to recognise and accept it than to let them be the cause of not working in this way with any class.

For most classes, however, different aptitudes and characteristics can be catered for in the way we design the work that we give them to do. There may be pupils who are shy and inhibited as well as those who, initially at least, find the self-discipline that we require of them difficult to master. There are also those who are deliberately disruptive. For this final set we need to find a realistic way of working which does not give them the opportunity for further disruption which will lead to chaos. Wilfully disruptive pupils can be a problem for any teacher. Unless you are sure that these pupils will be motivated by the work, you will create difficulties in leaving them to work on their own. In the long run the whole class will benefit by adopting an approach which takes account of them, even if this means delaying the start of group work as a method. Before you feel that any such pupils are causing the work of the rest of the class to suffer it is vital that you refer the problem to senior colleagues. This is not a sign of failure. Normal departmental structuring within schools makes provision for dealing with problems of this nature. It will only be in situations where there is a lack of sympathy from colleagues about this method that there might be a real problem. If you are the only music teacher in the school and are new and having these problems, it will be helpful for senior colleagues to have a clear understanding of the particular difficulties of applying group work to the teaching of music.

Other sets of pupils include those who are apathetic and not easy to motivate, and those who are keen but find their work difficult. Again, there are those pupils who have musical training on an instrument, usually accompanied by a knowledge of notation, who sometimes find it hard to let go of their traditional training in an attempt to be creative. We must be very careful that we don't undermine but enhance their musical ability by expanding it through creative work.

II: *Planning versatile work*

It is not possible to give a perfect recipe for dealing with classes of different complexions since these, in combination with the character of the teacher, are so many and various. We can though give some hints about what to bear in mind when planning work for such a complex combination of individuals. None of us can possibly design thirty different lessons with up to six groups in each class every week, so we have to find work which is sufficiently adaptable to be applicable to a number of different classes and abilities at once. The particular task that you expect the class to perform in any lesson must be attainable in some degree by all groups within the class. We must look therefore at designing lessons which are suitable for groups of different complexities in different classes. Teachers following the courses of work in the previous chapter must find introductory and complementary material which is suitable and applicable to all groups of pupils; otherwise the constant demand for individually tailored work will become too great, and impossible to achieve. All options must have a versatility in their interpretation so that groups of pupils can home in on a level which is suitable to them.

Later in this chapter we will look at the particular considerations that need to be made when drawing up lesson plans for group work, using our lesson plan structure from the previous chapter. Before this, however, it might be useful to examine particular requirements of certain pupils with respect to this work.

Most first-year pupils are willing and enthusiastic and enjoy composing their own music. However, we must recognise that there will be some individuals in some classes who for various reasons fall outside this group. As this kind of work requires a personal contribution from the pupils, we must be prepared to understand the needs and cater for those who do not instantly and enthusiastically respond. This is *particularly* important when we want them to work in groups where they are away from our constant attention. We will look at some typical characteristics and suggest ways of coping with them, but we must stress that these are just suggestions, not prescriptions. New teachers, however, can perhaps take heart from the knowledge that we all have, at some time, pupils who are difficult to accommodate.

The diffident and less confident pupils

Ensure that neither you nor the demands of the work deny them the degree of privacy within which they feel comfortable. Let them work with the people whom they choose. It is quite common for these pupils to want to work with more extrovert characters. They can do this even though at first they may be dominated. In this case ensure that they have specific tasks to accomplish, the achievement of which may help to promote more confidence. Alternatively they often choose to work together. You need to ensure their protection so that their work can flourish; we must not confuse a lack of confidence with apathy or lack of ability. Don't force the group to perform to the rest of the class; let them begin by performing to one other individual and then perhaps to another group. Encourage the taping of performances and let the pupils' confidence in performance grow at its own pace. It might take all year – or more. For those who particularly lack confidence in the worth of their composing ideas, we must be extra sensitive about criticism and err on the side of generosity to bring out as much as we can, but also try to develop in them a sense of self-criticism, as this diffidence should not mask a lack of effort.

Pupils who at first lack the self-discipline to work in groups

For these pupils we must keep a fairly rigorous control over the activities we set them to do. Many shorter, precise tasks are preferable to one long open-ended activity. These pupils need a clear structure to their work and we can give them increasingly complex tasks. We are not talking here about wilfully disobedient pupils but those who treat being out of their teacher's eye as an opportunity to play about. These pupils need to see that work which they do on their own will meet with enthusiasm and encouragement when they bring it back to us. It is a regenerative process which is best begun with simple tasks which are quickly rewarded for those who are less able. The more able among this set of pupils still need the structure and the rewards, but require demanding tasks which match their level of ability. You will cause more disruption among these pupils if you underestimate the complexity of the tasks which they require to satisfy their ability. Even though they may need to acquire the early, more simple composing skills, these need to be *presented* in a way that is a challenge to their intellect. Much disruption can be unwittingly caused in classes by pupils who are underachieving.

The apathetic and those lacking motivation

There tend to be two groups of such pupils. First, there are those who are quite capable academically but who seem completely unable to translate their ability into an expressive medium. These pupils will invariably be those who in the rest of their school life are able to succeed by first learning the minimum required and then relying on their native ability for the rest. They know and understand the system; and are able to achieve the necessary goals. When we require them to operate in a system whose rules of success they may not understand because of its newness to them, coupled with their preconceived ideas of what music *should* be, their defence in the face of failure is to opt out. These pupils may lack respect for us because they do not understand our system of measuring achievement, and they take the view that we are supervising an activity in which success is not in direct relation to intellectual ability. This is indeed the case but for these pupils we must be more open in explaining the reasons for what we are doing with them, as well as our system for recognising achievement. Until they can accept that their composing work is as rigorous a test of their aptitude as the demands of other areas of the curriculum, then these pupils are likely to opt out of the activity since the alternative is to submit themselves to a position in which they believe they are vulnerable. Our duty to these pupils is to show them that there are different ways of developing their abilities, not all of which are measurable by grades of rightness and wrongness. We can show them that self-expression can be a powerful and important part of their character. The confidence they gain through their own powers of self-expression sits comfortably with intellect, and we must give them the chance to experience this. So, when designing work for these pupils, we need to identify the root of their reluctance to participate, being prepared to discuss this with them and devise work suitable for them.

Secondly, there are those pupils who are difficult to motivate and are apathetic generally in their school life, and no less so in their music lessons. It is obviously worth checking with colleagues that this is the case with particular pupils. It can be very difficult to know what to do with them. They tend not to be deliberately disruptive or intrusive, but rather sit out the lesson with the barest minimum of input and interest. They will usually do what is required of them, but without imagination and energy. In a busy classroom, where demands on our attention are great, the uninterested and indifferent pupil can easily be overlooked. We find that these pupils more than any others need a lot of personal attention. If we get to know them a bit better they can sometimes be motivated to work out of respect for us as their teachers, and this can lead to an enjoyment in the work for its own sake. Sometimes success can be forthcoming if they are encouraged to work within an enthusiastic group. Giving them work on their own with short spells of personal attention can also bring rewards and will break up the potential spread of apathy through a group of likeminded pupils. There are no simple solutions to dealing with these pupils; they are probably the most difficult and challenging set for us to cope with in composing activities which rely so strongly on an active exploring mind.

Pupils who have formal musical training on an instrument

These are another special group for us to consider, particularly in the context of a musically mixed-ability class. Pupils are usually organised into classes either of completely mixed ability or streamed according to their abilities in other subjects. We are likely therefore to have a few pupils in any class who have a degree of technical ability and theoretical knowledge from instrumental tuition. With these pupils we must bear in mind a number of things. It could be that for them it is best to find a way of expanding their musical experience which uses their skills as a starting-point. We have found that sometimes pupils who are established players can get trapped within the world of music they understand. When it comes to composing, their idea of a composer is usually the person who has written *their* music and often early attempts at composing are confined to an imitation of this. For some this is very successful, particularly where their established skill is in a 'pop' style. Pupils more familiar with classical styles in their repertoire get more disheartened when their attempts to emulate these styles in composition fail. These pupils may need to be encouraged to explore other possibilities on their instrument and on other instruments. They may need to learn how to compose without necessarily having to notate and without the specific structure of a given form. As they are adept at playing their instrument, improvisation on this will be a valuable source of composing ideas and therefore an important skill to develop. An encouraging starting-point for them is to ask them to create a piece which is designed to display their particular skills on their instrument. These pupils can be encouraged in the early stage of the music course to work on their own instruments and to translate their knowledge onto other instruments. You can achieve tremendous results in a composing course if a group of instrumentalists work together. We must be careful, particularly when introducing work to a class, that we don't undermine or underestimate the competence of these pupils, who are usually in the minority in most schools. In the work we prepare for them we must stretch and challenge and develop their musicianship without belittling or ignoring it. They will feel that music is *their* subject and will be willing to succeed if we manage to convince them that what we are doing is as new and as big a challenge to them as it is to the rest of the class.

II: *Grouping*

The groups of pupils we have discussed above are not necessarily the groups we would expect to find working together in the classroom. Before moving on to group work we need to consider the grouping of pupils for work since this will have an important effect on its success. Initially we strongly recommend allowing pupils to choose their own groups but restricting the number according to our purposes. We do not want to create friction, and we want the pupils to be in a comfortable context to work. Only severe character clashes should be the reason for changing the members of a group at the beginning.

‖: *Encouraging fluidity/Re-arranging the groups*

As work progresses other considerations and good reasons present themselves for re-arranging members of groups, and it is obviously best to explain these to pupils before making changes. It is often the case that there is a particular sympathy in ideas and styles of music between certain pupils, and we might feel that it is better for these pupils to work together. As the class become accustomed to working, and generally become more secure in sharing their ideas, it is essential to encourage more fluidity between groups so that the greatest possible exchange of ideas can take place. It is worth trying to encourage boys and girls to work together, but not really worth pressing if they find this inhibiting, as they often do. There seems to come a time when this barrier disappears naturally and the musical considerations take precedence in the *pupils'* minds in selecting their groups.

‖: *Organising according to musical ability*

You may feel it beneficial after a while to re-organise groups according to individual pupils' musical ability. Beware of keeping a group of very-low-ability pupils together. Their input may have come from working with a more able pupil whom you have chosen to put into another setting. At times you *will* want the less able pupils together in order to spend some time with them, but it is best not to have the class grouped according to ability levels all the time. Pupils can learn a lot from each other and the less able can often be motivated by classmates more successfully than by us. Always give a positive musical reason for moving pupils so that they enter the new group with the feeling that they have been moved there for the contribution they can make to it.

‖: *Individual work*

Finally, it is always important to remember that there will be some pupils who choose and are very positive about wanting to work on their own. There is no harm in this if they are happy working in this way, once you are satisfied that there are musical reasons for their wanting to do this.

‖: *Introducing group work*

The way we begin group work is likely to vary given the different make-up of each class, as is the timing of the decision about when to begin. There are various ways of introducing group work, which depend upon the ability of your class to cope with working in this way. You may want to begin with group activities which familiarise the pupils with the idea of working in groups, but without the instruments to start with. It might be helpful to get some insight into the way the class works in groups in other lessons from their drama or English teachers, for example, or to organise these types of activities for yourself. (There are some good drama publications, which have preparatory exercises for group work, listed at the end of this book.)

II: *The first lesson*

It is very important that the first composing group work session is a *success* – that is, it is an enjoyable and engaging activity for the majority of pupils. This will not be the case if proper preparation has not been made and due consideration given to the timing and readiness of the class to work in this way. Once you feel that you are ready to try composing using group work, you may want to introduce it by setting off one group at a time. This makes it a more controllable activity at the beginning. It gives us the opportunity to see how well any group of pupils can cope with the self-discipline required if we set up a core class activity from which groups break to work on their own. We can stagger the splitting of the class and recall any groups to a central activity if necessary.

II: *Observation*

In relation to the course plans of the previous chapter, we would expect to spend the first term observing how the pupils work in pairs for composing, and in groups for non-composing activities. This will give us some insight into how the pupils are likely to work in groups for composing. But as an extra control, staggering the beginnings is a method which is especially helpful when dealing with a large class. The following lesson plan shows one way of putting this into operation.

SAMPLE LESSON   Wood, skin, metal and string

Introduction

The aim is to create a class composition which highlights contrast of instruments made of different materials. Pupils using electronic keyboards can select sounds from within particular families of instruments. The piece will have the structure of either A B A C A D, etc. or A B C D C B A, where A is the class playing together and B, C, D, etc. are groups.

Preparation   If there is no space available outside the main classroom area, the room needs to be organised in such a way that the pupils can be together at the beginning of the lesson and able to move away in groups as the lesson progresses.

Instruments   Have the instruments set out in 'families' ready for use. If you have several of one type of instrument which has a variety of timbres within itself – for example cymbals, electronic keyboards – use these for one group.

Grouping   Ask the pupils to organise themselves into groups. (We suggest no more than five in a group at this stage.) This is probably better done in the previous lesson so that when they arrive they can go straight to the sets of instruments which you allocate to them.

The lesson

The lesson begins by composing section A, which is the whole class playing together. Individuals can compose patterns which they repeat or improvise. We suggest that this section is played quietly and continuously to produce a gentle 'wash' of sound. From this, distinct sections will emerge, each of which will be played by a different group of instruments. These will need to be composed separately by each group.

Group activity   Still with the whole class together, explain that they are going to compose sections which contrast with the sounds of section A. Select one of the families or sets of instruments and ask the pupils who are playing these to demonstrate the particular qualities of timbre. Involve the class in suggesting different methods of playing. The groups will need to think about structuring their sections and we can help them to do this by suggesting a number of features around which they can plan their work. We want to hear the distinctive timbres of particular instruments in contrast to the mixture of sounds of section A, so a strong rhythmic pattern, contrasting dynamics, or more definition in playing in a decisive style, are devices to which we can draw their attention.

This group can now move away from the class to compose their section while you concentrate on the same preparation for each set of instruments in turn.

Performing and listening   Once all the sections are completed the class can listen to each group's composition in turn and decide on the best order for them to be played. The original plan is to play the whole piece in the form A B A C, etc. but if the music lends itself, or the class favour a different structure, then this may well be preferable.

‖: *The practical problems of group work*

There are three common practical problems associated with group work organisation:

1 It will quickly become apparent, particularly in a mixed-ability class, that groups work at different speeds.
2 Groups distributed in outside classrooms and in practice rooms are difficult to monitor.
3 A number of groups working in one room can become difficult to control.

The second and third of these are such common and central problems to this course that we examine them in the next chapter. The first one we will look at here.

‖: *Groups working at different speeds*

The most important point in this situation is that the group who take the longest must be given time to finish their work. It is quite common that these are the more able pupils who often want to spend more time working through their ideas and perfecting their performance. This is a good sign in terms of their learning process. We can treat this situation positively by giving these groups the time and independence that they need, assisting them when they require it so that groups who are finding the work difficult or who finish quickly can be given more regular help with a variety of new materials and ideas. This forms the central part of the teacher's role in the activity. It will only be possible though if either we feel confident enough to give them new ideas spontaneously, or (and this really ought to be the case) we have sufficient alternative material. Again, knowing what is likely to happen given the pupils in your class, is the best preparation for this.

‖: *Concentration span*

It is very important to recognise that some pupils and groups of pupils cannot concentrate on composing for as long as others. There is no point in persisting once their concentration is exhausted. It is best to change the activity. With pupils such as these there is a strong case for having an integrated music course. In this way these pupils' needs are quite compatible with those who can concentrate and want to work on composing for longer spells.

II: *Preparing alternative activities*

If we look, for example, at the plan for Year 1 Term 3 of the thematic course outlined in the previous chapter (page 58), the composing activity – *using a poem as a stimulus for composition* (see pages 38–45) – may be completed much sooner by some groups than others. If we have the other activities prepared – a large task for us for the first two years but worthwhile in the long run – our pupils can move on to other activities. They could, for example, find out about King Arthur and Merlin as background to *The Lady of Shalott*. We may want them to do some illustrative work for part of an integrated project display, or to practise some easy arrangements of medieval music. If the work can be organised in this way it is a positive sign of achievement in that the needs of a mixed-ability class are being catered for, and that composing is among these needs. It may not be because of problems that we organise work in this way; indeed, we might decide that it is more stimulating for the pupils to have different activities going on at once.

II: *Styles of group work*

Groups can work on compositions in different ways. We usually think of a group composition as one which is created by all the pupils of the group collectively for a combination of their instruments/voices. We would expect this to be the case early on when the individual's composing skills are limited. This is the context, once group work has been established, within which most of our first year and a lot of subsequent work will be done.

There are, however, other ways that a group can produce a composition and it is important where possible to encourage this variety as it gives individuals the opportunity to expand their composing skills in different ways. With sophisticated keyboards or a piano, a small group can compose a piece for the one instrument. In this way they can get more out of a more complex instrument than they could individually. Keyboard players can work on pieces together, especially where their composing skills are not as developed as their playing skills. They might collectively compose a piece for solo performance by any of them, or one in which they all have a part to play.

Stuart directing a group composition

II: *Directing a group*

Another idea which has proved very successful is where one pupil directs a group to create her or his own composition. Pupils who are rich in musical ideas, who are confident in articulating these, and who are beginning to develop a power of conjecture, can be given the opportunity where this is possible and where it is a positive exercise for the rest of the group. There might be a case for including pupils in this group who do not have these facilities if it is felt that it will be of genuine help in developing them. Otherwise, make up the group with pupils who are capable of directing, giving each of them the opportunity to do so. A variation of this is where the members of the group contribute ideas for the composition but one member takes the final decisions in constructing the piece.

II: *The individual within the group*

It can be helpful as a departmental record to profile the way that individuals work with these different styles of composing as well as in different groupings. In conjunction with the assessment sheets (pages 52 and 53) this would give us a quite thorough overview of each pupil's response to the composing course. It might not be necessary or feasible to complete all the assessment sheets in every case, but assessment sheet 3 on page 78 is a further option. We have tried to reduce the numerous considerations to those which it is useful to record and which might assist colleagues. The function of this information is as a record and reminder of the placing and response of individual pupils within group work situations. Ideally, if this profiling can be collated at the end of the first year, it can help to provide a positive starting-point for the beginning of the second year of the course. Similar profiling can be appropriate from second year into third year. As with the assessment sheets in the previous chapter, we have designed the profile sheet so that it is easy and quick to complete, since for many of us there are a lot to do. Any consideration that teachers feel it is important to record about the individual within group work should be included.

Assessment sheet 3

Record of pupil's involvement in group work

Name of pupil..

Date	Composition	Type of assignment	Members of group
	A		
	B		
	C		
	D		
	E		

Assessment of pupil for each of these compositions (award grades 1 to 5)

	A	B	C	D	E

Did the pupil

○ contribute ideas?

○ direct any of the work?

○ contribute to the performance?

○ work constructively in this group?

Other observations

SONGS

The three songs on pages 80–86 were written by second-year groups. They are examples of three different approaches to song writing. Each song took about three double lessons to complete.

Timothy Winters

This group of six girls chose to set a poem to music. The performance was mainly directed by two members of the group but they all contributed ideas during composition.

Health Song

This was the result of a project which the class were doing in their social studies lessons. The group's aim was to compose music which would be compelling, and would get across a message about good health. Their composition arose out of improvisation of both words and music. They used electronic keyboards, guitars and percussion for the accompaniment.

The Rainbow Connection

This group chose to re-set existing lyrics to new music. Initially all the work was done vocally and the group added their chordal keyboard accompaniment once they had composed the melody. The piece on pages 87–88 was written by a girl after she had worked on *The Rainbow Connection*. Other examples of pupils' comments on group work are given on pages 118–125.

Timothy Winters

Verse 1. unaccompanied.

Ti-mo-thy Win-ters comes to school with

eyes as wide as a foot-ball pool,

Ears like bombs and teeth like splin-ters, a

blitz of a boy is Tim-o-thy Win-ters

Tim-o-thy Win-ters.

Verse 2.

Voices

Ti - mo-thy

Glockenspiel

Claves

Cello

He sleeps in a sack on the kit-chen floor and they say there aren't boys like him a-ny more, a-ny more, a-ny more a-ny more

Health Song

keyboard Gm

D7

improvise Bm   F#

Bm

If you think that health comes nat-ural-ly   well

F#

I've got news for you   If you

wan-na be a-live in two thou - sand and five

Bm

list-en to the things you should do

Cut out the fags and to-bacc-o   and

F#

pour the drink down the sink

cut out the grea-sy chips and things and
see what it does for you.

Bm x 4

Bm
Don't take drugs of a-ny kind you can
make it on your own take
lots of health-y ex-er-cise don't
let your bo-dy down.

Bm x 4

Bm
Gum and sweets just rot your teeth
they're no good at all. The
things you need are fruit and meat and
far less choco-late bars.

The Rainbow Connection

When you work in a group you all club together with loads more of good ideas.

It can also be fun learning and trying out new sounds with your group. I like composing in a group ~~with~~ that you can think up ideas together.

The most difficult part of composing was trying to get all the ideas into a good tune. The problems we had to overcome were fitting ideas in and discharging ideas.

The advantages of working in a group are you get more ideas and if someone can't play an instrument another person in the group will. The disadvantages of working in a group is you may get out voted and have to do something you didn't want to.

When you work on your own you use your own ideas and you don't have to do what any one else says. Sometimes though you can't think of ideas and

that's a great disadvantage.
I don't think I could compose
on my own I ~~need~~ need other
peoples ideas to get my brain
going. Music doesn't always
have to be written down but
sometimes it does help you to
remember your things.

I think the piece of music
which was most successful
was making up a tune to
songwords of 'The Rainbow
Connection'. We had lots of
fun trying to reach the high
and low notes of it.

The Rainbow Connection had
some good words to make up
a tune to.

II: *Checklist for preparing a lesson for group work*

II: *Preparation*

Content

○ Does the work cater for all levels of ability? Is the stimulus open to interpretation at all levels?

○ Are the objectives of the lesson clearly defined? Do these involve specific tasks or is the pupil's response to be more open-ended? Know which and stick to it.

○ Are you clear about where the lesson fits into a scheme of work so that groups who work quickly can move on?

○ Do you have sufficient complementary consolidating work where this is appropriate?

Resources

○ Have spaces and instruments prepared before the lesson.

○ Remember that certain instruments are more attractive to younger pupils who will choose them regardless of suitability. Make sure you know how these instruments will be allocated.

○ How much choice for the pupils is realistic, given the resources? Are the resources suitable for the activity?

○ Will you have to allocate the resources? If so, how will you do this?

○ Check the working order of instruments and plan positioning of power points, etc.

○ Have tape recording facilities prepared.

○ Make attractive, durable work cards, as these will build into a useful resource.

Groupings

○ Have these prepared as far as you can.

○ Pre-empt any possible conflicts in pupil choice.

○ Be ready to re-arrange any poor groupings which may not be apparent until work is under way.

○ Know the criteria which you are using for grouping.

○ Take previous or present absentees into account. (It is amazing how much havoc can be caused by a pupil returning to school.)

‖: *Introducing the work*

○ Although when introducing a topic to the whole class it will be on a more general level, try as far as possible to personalise the work so that individuals and groups *see its relevance* in terms of their own perspective. The skill of your introduction lies in your ability to speak meaningfully to the *whole* class.

○ Where it is not possible to introduce the work to the whole class (who would then respond by working in groups), you will need to discuss each group's work with them individually. This will probably be at the start of a lesson once the project is under way. All groups should be occupied while you are going round.

‖: *Group activity*

○ If the work demands that the pupils choose their instruments after your introduction, make sure that your method of distribution is quick and efficient.

○ As soon as groups begin working, get round them all quickly to make sure they know what they are doing. Then spend longer in observation (see Chapter 2).

‖: *Performing and listening*

○ Decide whether this is appropriate in the case of each lesson.

‖: *Instruments and space*

'It is helpful for the music *suite* to be associated with the hall or theatre . . . where the accommodation is not so comprehensive the programme of work will be determined by the possibilities of the teaching space available and the ingenuity of the teacher.'

(HMI document, *Music from 5 to 16*)

This chapter is for teachers whose working conditions fall short of ideal. The two most pressing problems with resources can be a lack of space in which to work, particularly with groups, and inadequate stocks of equipment in terms of quality, variety and suitability for this age group. The aim of this chapter is to explore ways of using what *is* available so that we can work despite limitations.

‖: *Space*

Those of us not housed in music suites are probably timetabled to work with full-sized Lower School classes in one room. We should never underestimate the constant determination and energy that music teachers need when trying to organise practical work in poor conditions. We must find ways of not letting the working situation become stressful in the face of our ideals; it should be a positive environment within which the pupils can work. Indeed, in a limited space great demands *are* made on our strength and ingenuity. If space is inadequate we have two options: either to organise the work in such a way that it can be done in the one room; or to secure some extra spaces nearby which groups can occupy. This latter option has its own problems which we shall look at later, but first we will explore the alternatives open to us if we have to be in the one room, as most of us do.

‖: *Working in one room*

Is the whole course planned to take account of the restriction of the one room only?

It is so disheartening to have an exciting project thwarted by some practical consideration which may have been overlooked. So in a world

Groups working in one room

that is not ideal, it is much better and more encouraging for us and the pupils if we do half a job well rather than the whole job badly. If it is not possible to have the whole class involved in practical group activities at once then we must organise the course to take account of that limitation. To do this we need to be absolutely clear about priorities. If we feel that at all costs pupils should have some experience of group-based composing activities, and feel that our *whole* music course should be practical, yet the whole class working in groups is an organisational impossibility, then we have to face a compromise. Either we organise lessons where the whole class is playing but not in groups, or we have only some groups playing at any one time with the others involved in non-practical activities. We must see this as *achieving* part of our aim rather than failing in it. But before we reject the possibility of groups working simultaneously in one room and devise other means of working, we still need to consider the next question.

II: *Classroom layout*

Can the allocation of furniture and its positioning within the room be adjusted to make whole class group work more feasible?

An imaginative layout of appropriate furniture (e.g. larger tables instead of sloping desks), can make a classroom more conducive to group work. Is there any way that separate working areas within the one room can be created using the furniture? This does not get round the problem of the noise, but it does help the pupils to feel that they are working in their own space. A compromise goal therefore is to have furniture which makes this possible. New teachers need to explain their requirements as it might be possible to swap desks for tables with another classroom where it makes no difference. What may seem obvious to us in terms of our classroom organisation, is not necessarily obvious to colleagues. Even if no change is possible, the problem has been registered with senior staff. An obvious tip if you are wanting different arrangements for different lessons is to get pupils, at the end of their lesson, to re-organise the room for the incoming class.

II: *Shorter working spells*

Is it possible to arrange the work so that the exploratory stages are divided into shorter spells?

In our experience it is not usually possible for five or six groups to work effectively at the same time on extended pieces in one room. They do, however, seem able to concentrate despite the noise for five- or

Class composition

ten-minute sessions. It seems that after this period the build-up of noise is too much and it gets frustrating for everyone. But we can utilise these shorter spells by breaking down the work into a more precise series of tasks which are interspersed with 'control' activities to give the pupils a rest from the accumulation of noise. It must be remembered that we are asking the pupils to produce creative work in an imperfect environment. We cannot do this unless our planning takes account of the limitations of their ability to cope. If the course requires longer periods of exploratory activity working in groups, then it will not usually be possible for them all to do the same thing at the same time, particularly at the beginning (though there will always be exceptional classes who can cope with the situation). So alternative methods of working need to be found.

II: *Staggering the activities*

Is it possible to arrange the composing activities so that the groups are at different stages?

A system can operate where after an introduction by the teacher to the whole class, there is a ten-minute session with everybody working. Thereafter one or two groups could continue working freely without any dynamic constraint whilst others consolidate their ideas through discussion, or plan a score. Groups can then take their turn in the more extended exploratory session; or in practising quietly (knowing they can use full dynamics in performance); or in discussing, listening to each other, and scoring. Once this rotation system is operating (and it will only do so successfully when the *pupils* understand that it is the best way you all have of organising the lesson), then they seem more ready to accept it. The paramount condition with this system is that the pupils *know* that they will ultimately have enough time to complete their composition. It does work if we are sensitive to the fluidity of the interchanging activities. If this seems to be the system that works best for you, the pupils will soon come to accept the routine, particularly if they know why and are *prepared* for the changes of activity at the beginning of the lesson.

II: *Noise control*

Finally, have all possible practical forms of control been explored?

Amid a noisy class we need clear, decisive signals which the pupils know they must instantly respond to as part of their routine. In a typical lively secondary school class, establishing control signals is a basic necessity. Find a signal, for example a single piano chord. Shouting just adds to the din!

If these methods of organising group work do not seem preferable or plausible – and there is no doubt that there can be drawbacks as well as advantages in this way of organising activities – then we need to examine other ways of organising composing activities with a class all together.

Alternatives are to organise lessons where the pupils do not work in groups, or to find non-practical activities so that only some groups are involved in practical activities at one time. A combination of these is probably the best way of getting round the problem.

II: *Whole class compositions*

We include here a sample lesson and ideas for song writing to show how whole class compositions can be created.

The Maze: Year 1 Term 1 *or* Year 2 Term 2

Class lessons should be devised so that all pupils can be involved in the composition and will contribute to the final performance. The starting-point should be an idea which is flexible enough to accommodate all abilities. In this lesson each of the pupils (or pairs or groups) chooses a character and composes a rhythmic pattern to represent it. Each of the characters will enter an imaginary maze and the class must decide the route and progress of each of them within the maze. For example, they may walk straight through it; get lost in it; go round in circles; walk and then rest; and so on. The piece must be structured so that the sounds represent all of this movement. It may end with all of the characters arriving at the centre either together or one at a time, or they could arrive at different times and work their way out again. If the centre of the maze is represented by one instrument which registers the arrival of the characters this instrument's playing will create a natural central or final section in the structure of the piece.

Musical aims

To create contrast and character through rhythmic patterns and to explore the textural effects of the combination and juxtaposition of these.

Preparation

Generally the pupils need to be able to see each other; so for this lesson we should have the class in a large circle.

Instruments

You may like to emphasise contrast through timbre as well as through rhythmic patterns. Alternatively, groups who choose to enter the maze together can use instruments of similar types.

The lesson

Activity After the teacher has explained the idea behind the composition, the pupils need time to choose a character and work on a rhythmic pattern to represent it. The class then listen to all the patterns of the people going into the maze. Collective decisions are made about particular features the class want to include. For example, groups meeting up and moving together, which groups will reach the centre, and will the centre of the maze signal the middle or the end of the piece? Other points to bear in mind when structuring the music are as follows:

- How will the characters enter – singly or in groups?
- How long will you spend on each character?
- How will you sustain the characters' progress through the maze to create an interesting texture in the music?
- What signals will you decide to use so that the pupils are clear about when they play?
- Will decisions about dynamics be spontaneous or directed?
- What balance will there be between improvised and rehearsed sections?

Performing and listening One important technique which the pupils are learning during this activity is to do with the art of performance. They must watch and respond to the person directing the music. Although when the pupils are playing they may be improvising, they are not individually structuring the piece. Both our experience with the class and their ability to articulate ideas will determine how much or how little we have to contribute to this process. If we are directing the final performance we must contribute only as much as we think necessary to produce a good piece which shows varieties of texture and a thought-out structure. Repeating and practising sections gives pupils the chance to be critical about their part in the final performance and to modify their contribution if they need to. It is good to reinforce ideas by repetition and let the class enjoy the familiar sound of the music which they have rehearsed. Some pupils can cope with directing the music themselves.

Song writing: Year 1 Term 3

The following are suggestions of ways to approach song writing as a whole class activity. We have found that classes like to work in different ways. The ideas here are, therefore, a collection of observations rather than a single lesson plan.

To begin with, you need to decide whether to tackle the words alone first or the words and music together.

Exchanging ideas

Lyrics first

You can write the words together as a class, or groups can each write different sets themselves. Suggest some possible subjects for lyrics. Make up a work card for each group bearing in mind the following points.

○ Strong rhythm in the words might be helpful.
○ Full sentences are not essential.
○ Words, phrases or lines can be repeated – this can sometimes help in structuring the song.
○ Nonsense lines can be included, for example *boo - be - doo*, etc.
○ A chorus, even wordless, can be a binding mechanism.

When enough groups have written their lyrics the class need to decide which ones they are going to use. (Groups whose words are not used can compose the music on another occasion.) Ideas can sometimes be combined. From here there are various starting-points into the music.

Lyrics and music together

From individual suggestions, decide on important musical features for the song, for example:

○ style, tempo, mood
○ strong rhythmic features
○ chords or chord progressions
○ possible improvisation by singing or playing an opening melody or a melody for the chorus

It is a good idea for the whole class to try out ideas together. They usually know immediately when they have found an idea that works. Somebody sings or plays a bar or so which you repeat – keep repeating this until more is forthcoming. Teach the class these few opening bars. If more ideas are not offered, suggest something yourself. Some classes find it easier to reject your ideas and substitute their own than to start from cold. It might help to switch back and forth between ideas for the chorus and for the verse. Certainly to begin with, it is best if the class work through each idea together in turn so that, for example, melody, rhythm and chord progressions are worked on by everybody.

When there is a consensus about a melody and possible accompaniments, different pupils can practise the parts they will be performing. This works for five or ten minutes, at which point we can put together what we have so far. Hereafter we need to repeat the process until the song is completed – this may involve changing parts, adjusting the words, and so on.

When the song is composed, other instrumental accompaniments or vocal variations can be added.

Echoes

This idea, a familiar one to many music teachers, works particularly well with the more gregarious and adventurous classes. The class gather in small groups at various points around the room. The music is initially improvised, and the piece is created by exploiting the musical effects of passing and developing themes from one space to another across the room. Anything from single notes to longer phrases can be echoed between the groups. Recipient groups can develop the theme as it is passed to them, perhaps by changing the rhythm, tempo, dynamics and so on. First, though, we need to come up with some simple rules about who is going to play, and when. You may decide that the best plan is to direct the groups from the centre before going on to more spontaneous improvisation. This is a lesson which is excellent for helping to develop listening skills through performance and developing sharp, spontaneous responses to on-the-spot musical instructions. It's also great fun. Classes who can work well with this idea could go on to compose and rehearse a piece using these kinds of spatial effects. If we are also doing group work with the class the ideas can be used in this situation. As a class exercise it does go some way towards giving individuals and groups the chance to use more of their own ideas.

Quiet music

Any lesson ideas which concentrate on composing music using quiet dynamics and silence can obviously be more easily adapted as whole class lessons. Stimuli which we know will produce quiet music or work which concentrates on this as an end in itself is, understandably, more containable in a smaller space. (Try the project on Silence, project 6, in Paynter and Aston's book *Sound and Silence*, Cambridge University Press, 1970.)

II: *Limitations of whole class composition*

This method of composition can be a very strong complement to group work. If group work proves impossible, then at least class composition does give pupils some opportunity to be involved in composing. However, if our composing course can only be devised for whole classes working together, then we must be aware of the limitations. There is less scope for the more extended involvement of group work or solo composing. The way to compensate for this is to give the pupils reasonable time to explore their ideas as they surface.

There is the obvious limitation that the educational and musical aims of group work cannot be satisfied. Indeed, the pupils will not have the opportunity for the privacy and the independence of extended periods of exploration. There is also the possibility that enthusiastic and co-opera-tive members of a class will have their efforts curtailed by having to work in a situation with others who are less co-operative and willing. We need to weigh up, as much as with group work, the feasibility of pursuing this activity with each class, especially where there are disruptive pupils.

The teacher's role differs slightly in this activity in that it is central and co-ordinating, in dealing with all members of the class at one time. We are less free to devote time to individual pupils. It is therefore imperative that when planning we cater for pupils who are unwilling to participate. Another point we must consider when planning to use this method over an extended period is that there may be a limitation in the amount of material that is suitable for working in this way, *particularly* with a mixed-ability class. Nor will it be possible to make the kinds of detailed individual assessment that we would hope to make with group work. From our own point of view we must feel confident that we can cope with the influx of ideas and deal with the compromises that we will have to make. We need to be able to combine our two roles of musical co-ordinator and class organiser. As well as this we have to be sensitive to the potential problem of accommodating less confident or inhibited pupils.

However, despite these considerations, composing with the whole class together can be a very good way of exploring the composing process. If group work is really not possible within the music lesson it can motivate some pupils to further interest outside the classroom situation. We ought perhaps to consider offering composing workshops as part of our extra-curricular programme.

II: *Sending groups out*

The alternative when working with limited accommodation is to try to secure odd spaces outside the music room in which groups can work. The classic example is the broom cupboard, but we have used the school field, the headteacher's office, and the changing rooms – the possibilities are endless. However, to secure even these you may need some bargaining power – packets of banda paper and loans of extension leads are common currency!

For new teachers contemplating sending groups out: this can be the ideal solution, but do not do it unless you have ascertained the following:

○ You have the approval of the headteacher.

Composing with keyboards

○ You have the acknowledged understanding and preferably the sympathy of colleagues nearby who may be affected by the noise.

○ You are as sure as you can be that the behaviour of pupils sent out will be defensible and you are prepared to accept the risks and implications of a misjudgement.

○ You have equipped the pupils with a set of specific tasks written on a work card and have given them a time limit.

○ You have organised the classroom activity so that you can regularly circulate among these groups and have the energy to do so.

For the sake of the work it is worth trying to do this, but it does involve a degree of co-operation and trust which must not be under-estimated. Fortunately, since current philosophy recognises that practical work is at the heart of music education, we now have an even stronger case for demanding recognition of this in the timetabling of our subject.

II: *Instruments*

Any practical course is totally dependent upon resources of equipment. The pupils must have a variety of good-quality instruments if they are to work seriously. If you have only a *few* good instruments, then these – and only these – must be the starting-point. You might have enough for only one group to work properly at any one time. Don't be tempted to use old, battered instruments in an enthusiasm to get everybody playing, as this will create problems. The pupils will quickly and understandably become dissatisfied with unresponsive instruments. In schools where there are not enough instruments we must be realistic about what is feasible and only work well within the limits of what is available. In such cases, the course of work which we propose is not possible for the whole class; but lessons and ideas can still be adapted for single group activities within an integrated course. We do not necessarily need a vast array of elaborate instruments in order to begin, but as well as variety there is a minimum number of instruments required if work with a whole class is to be effective. (There are suggested lists of these in the HMI document *Music from 5 to 16* and in John Paynter's *Music in the Secondary School Curriculum*, Cambridge University Press, 1982.) First and second years will happily use good classroom percussion instruments alongside more sophisticated electronic keyboards, guitars, etc.

II: *Requisition*

Teachers involved in allocating the music department budget face the perennial problem of balancing the specialist needs of examination classes, choirs, orchestras, bands, other music groups, school shows and concerts, with those of the day-to-day classroom in which we might have to cater for every pupil in the first three years. Even providing ourselves with an adequate stock in the first place is not the end of the problem, as the wear and tear on the instruments when running a practical course is not negligible.

II: *Percussion instruments*

We should look for a moment at the case for keeping stocks of good percussion instruments in these days of increasingly sophisticated electronic alternatives. There is no doubt that the widespread use of electronic keyboards has opened up tremendous possibilities for music in schools. We want to take full advantage of these, and also offer pupils attractive alternative instruments which they can play easily. Many people today associate tuned classroom percussion instruments with Orff and primary school work, and don't see how they can be taken seriously by secondary school pupils, particularly when there are such good electronic instruments available. However, in our experience of various comprehensive schools, we have found many pupils who respond well to a good-quality metallophone or xylophone as part of a *variety* of resources available to them. These, *in conjunction with* electronic instruments, professional untuned percussion, and any full-size band or orchestral instruments (a cymbal on a stand, a set of professional maracas and a keyboard prove popular with Lower School pupils who can readily identify with these instruments), are an acceptable combination to the pupils. Whatever we offer must have appeal in its own right and must not be the poor alternative.

CHAPTER FIVE

‖: *The third year*

‖: *A realistic view*

All practising teachers know that the third year can be difficult. Here we have a group of pupils who are at the end of a ten-year period of a broad-based curriculum in which music has usually been a compulsory subject. *We* might think this is a good thing, but for some of them, frankly, it is obviously wearing a bit thin. So what do we do? We want to continue to give them a stimulating course of work, and we want them all to continue to experience and enjoy practical music making. It is too disheartening – and a terrible waste of energy – to devise a superb scheme of work, involving composing, *on the assumption* that every third-year pupil will be keen and willing to participate. Many teachers will recognise the third-year pupils whose blatant disregard for the subject is second only to their need to be as obtrusive as possible in the classroom. Though their numbers may be small, their presence is very great. And we all know the class where these pupils are still being timetabled with the able and enthusiastic few, to say nothing of the amiable majority.

Any realistic discussion of a third-year programme must take into account the possibility of these extremes. We have previously referred to the situation where differences of ability and attitude exist in one class. By the third year such differences have often become acute. The enthusiasm of the keener pupils is now at its peak. Their skills and interests have developed during the past two years and they are at the stage when they can involve themselves in quite sophisticated independent project work.

‖: *Opting out*

As well as a course which needs to take account of these extremes, we need to provide for the great diversity of interests and abilities which have been developed. Composing will be only one of these interests because, by the third year, pupils are usually clear that they do or do not want to continue to be involved in composing. What this means in practice is that in any third-year class we are likely to have able and less able composers as well as those who do not want to be involved.

Another consideration in the third year is the pupils' own aspirations with regard to GCSE. For the non-composers this will not be an option; but for the composers it may be, regardless of their ability. One reason why pupils opt out of composing is that they have not been able, or have not wanted to develop any practical or playing skills beyond the initial stages, and this has inevitably thwarted the composing process. For them, music, and more particularly composing, it not a natural form of expression. There are also those pupils who do not enjoy practical work in any form, or just don't like music.

There seems to be little point in any of these pupils pursuing a composing course if it is to become a negative exercise for everyone concerned. As they will not be going into a fourth-year examination set, it will be more positive and pleasant if, in their last year of music, we can develop interests which they find more appealing. We must make individual judgements which balance our general aim: for all pupils to enjoy and get as much as they can from a school music course, with a recognition of the personal tastes and autonomy which are so particularly relevant in a creative area. Obviously, we shall want to take each pupil as far as we can, but we *must* leave the activity if a perpetual sense of failure, boredom or antagonism is setting in. However, when we are thinking of ways of working with the composers, we must always have in mind the alternative needs of these non-composers.

With first- and second-year pupils many of us will feel that there is a strong case for expecting them to become involved in *all* aspects of their course work. Having done that the third-year course should offer more flexibility of choice. Apart from the fact that a third-year pupil can be far more doggedly resistant to any insistence on our part, many of us recognise that, when limits are reached, we cannot and should not try to force expression through composition. As long as we are satisfied that the pupil has had sufficient encouragement and opportunity to be musically creative in the first and second years, if music is then rejected as a means of expression we must let it lie. What must not happen in this event is for teacher or pupil to feel a failure; or for the door to be permanently closed.

It is most unlikely that an average third-year class will be full of keen composers. Therefore we must be realistic and not simply assume that it will be or indeed should be otherwise. With this in mind, we need to look at ways of incorporating composing into the third-year programme for those who do want to continue with this option. Before exploring ideas for course work, we need to consider in more detail the various skills, aspirations and abilities of those pupils in an average third-year class.

II: *Some pupils*

Here we should like to introduce some different but, we think, typical third-year pupils from our own classes. We are sure that some of them will be familiar characters to most teachers. Later we will look at ways of structuring a third-year programme which take account of their very different needs. These pupils all enjoy music and want to continue with composing in one way or another. At the end of each description we give a brief summary of their responses to the first- and second-year course, and from this we try to define their needs. Thus, we hope to build up a picture of the points to be kept in mind when planning third-year schemes of work.

Andrew

Andrew, although an obliging pupil, does not manage to achieve a great deal in the course of his day. He spends most of his time with the support team as he is of very low ability. Music is compulsory, and along with cooking, metalwork and woodwork, is a favourite activity. Andrew has no developed instrumental or aural skills, but he does have a very acute sense of rhythm. When he comes to his music lesson he wants to work on the electronic keyboards; anything else (except drumming) is a poor substitute. Despite his lack of playing skill he has a considerable capacity (as seems quite common with poor-ability pupils) for going over and over snatches of his ideas until he is satisfied. Incidentally, this capacity extends to his wanting to learn well-known tunes. It would not be an exaggeration to say that he has spent many *hours* learning the first few bars of the 'EastEnders' theme tune. He likes to compose songs but needs a lot of help getting the words together. The development of his composing skills is very slow. All advice and help must be of the moment and immediately applicable.

Summary
o   little development in playing skills
o   enjoys and can persevere with simple composing skills, e.g. melodic ideas, making up rhythms
o   can match words to music
o   has benefited from group work; although he lacks the confidence to contribute his own ideas he enjoys playing a part as a member of a group
o   is not able to cope with abstract ideas
o   does not respond to descriptive stimuli

Needs
o   to build on the limited skills so far developed
o   to find ways of bringing together the skills he has
o   to build confidence in his own ideas so that he can develop his contribution to joint projects
o   careful supervision perhaps reinforced by use of the tape recorder
o   to establish links between his composing and other parts of his music course

Jane

Jane is quiet and reserved in the classroom. Her performance is below average across the curriculum. Her strongest musical interest is in singing and taking part in school productions. She has good aural skills and has started to develop an interest in the keyboard. Although her playing skills are developing, she is not very imaginative and does not have much confidence in her own ideas. She needs a lot of coaxing and really enjoys performing her own pieces once she has been persuaded that her ideas are worth pursuing.

Summary
o   responds best to step-by-step instructions, e.g. benefits from the support of work cards
o   takes a part in group compositions but is less forceful than others in contributing original ideas
o   is not adventurous or curious in experimenting with sounds
o   has limited interest in instruments other than keyboards, piano and voice
o   works best as one of a pair in composing activities

Needs
o   to develop playing skills alongside composing skills (*she* doesn't believe she can compose before she can play)
o   to be given composing work that is based on what she can already do
o   to develop further her ability to sing well and in harmony
o   to develop the confidence to be more imaginative and experimental
o   stimuli that are based on mood rather than visual stimuli
o   to be given composing work of which she can readily see the relevance – this probably means in the context of wider musical or creative arts projects

Peter

Peter spends most of his spare time in school composing music, usually pop songs, with his friends. All his work is improvised on keyboards. He is not at all interested in the conventions of musical theory though he does read music and plays the E flat bass in the school band. He has an instinctive sense of harmony and composes tunes with enviable ease. Composing and performing his own work is his favourite musical activity. He is generally thought of as having average ability in most subjects.

Summary
- o playing skills have improved dramatically
- o enjoys group work as a way of composing but at times finds it difficult when it means compromising his own ideas
- o good at directing a group with imaginative ideas
- o strong on improvisation
- o composing channelled into pop

Needs
- o to work on more sophisticated structure
- o to broaden his experience of style both within and outside pop
- o to learn to arrange his pieces for a wider variety of instruments (e.g. brass)
- o to be given more challenging stimuli
- o to explore the relationships between the arts (he is very interested in poetry and drama)
- o to develop more theoretical knowledge through *composing* (we think this will help him)
- o a lot of time and freedom to work alone but also teacher support

Lisa

Although generally Lisa's academic ability is comparable with Peter's, musically they are very different. She is fascinated by the mechanics of musical theory and has the capacity and inclination to listen to classical music for very long stretches. This interest is a challenge to her since it has long outstripped her playing skills. She is intrigued by the structure of music she hears, and has an unusually developed keenness to analyse it. Because her practical skills are so weak (and she has little interest in developing them), her approach to composing tends to be mechanical. Her main achievement, which she greatly enjoys, is composing melodies by humming them and then writing them down in staff notation as she goes along.

Summary
- keen to be involved in music but unimaginative and rather inhibited in practical work, though she likes to be part of a group and finds this supportive
- finds playing skills difficult but gets very involved with listening and background work
- she wants to learn about composing, although she is stronger on other aspects of the music course and seems more interested to find out how composing 'works' than to involve herself in the creative experience

Needs
- to be encouraged to believe that her own compositions are of intrinsic worth
- the facility to expand into unnotated compositions
- to work on one of the more sophisticated keyboards, preferably with headphones (because we think she needs privacy to experiment and develop)
- composing activities which relate to the background and listening which she enjoys

Matthew

His main musical passion is heavy rock. Out of school he has his own band in which he sings and plays guitar. When he was younger he was head chorister of a cathedral choir though he has never really mastered music reading. He says he might get around to it one day but doesn't see it as a necessity. His composing interests are through his band and in school he composes by improvising on guitar and keyboards. He is full of good ideas for compositions but seems to tire of them, often before he has seen them through.

Summary
- has shown flare, imagination and enthusiasm in composing
- has participated in the course for the first two years but has always been quite vocal about his likes and dislikes
- only co-operated in group work if he could choose and control his group, and would only work with people as musically able as himself; he likes to work on his own

○ skills have been developed erratically, and without applying himself to learning methodically; it has all been a bit haphazard but has produced some really good work

Needs

○ to find a way of harnessing and directing his skills without stifling his enthusiasm because we sense that he would get great satisfaction from completing a substantial piece of work
○ to initiate his own projects and to see them through
○ to improve his playing skills (he works well through improvisation)
○ to use information about musical relationships, e.g. key relations, chord composition, song structures, etc.

Thomas and Oliver

Thomas passed Grade V singing in his second year, and he plays the piano and tenor horn. He has a good theoretical knowledge and is very well informed about many styles of music. He spends a lot of his own time composing songs and organising his friends to perform them with him. In school he likes to experiment with sounds and can do so totally unconstrained by the styles of his musical training. He is very receptive to ideas and is full of initiative.

Oliver is an exceptionally gifted pupil academically; he is very strong in all subjects. He has already passed Grade V cello and during his third year he will be taking Grade VIII piano. He is a versatile and gifted musician who is able to work with a variety of instruments and musical styles in composition. Because of his technical skill and good ear he is able to imitate all kinds of musical styles well. His tendency therefore is to produce clever musical pastiche.

Summary

○ they have made the most of all aspects of the first two years' work
○ they have a good grasp of the elements of composition which they have explored through the course, and they are now able to work independently using this knowledge
○ they are able to respond to all kinds of stimuli and can now formulate their own ideas for composition and can see them through
○ Thomas's compositions are often less sophisticated in technique but more original in style than Oliver's

○   Thomas, unlike Matthew, is sensitive to other people's ideas and is happy to work in a group as well as on his own
○   by the end of the second year, Oliver was usually working on his own though he did enjoy group work up until that time

Need
○   to extend their understanding of the different systems and styles of music, e.g. tonality, structure, instrumentation
○   to see the potential of using established techniques in conjunction with their own experimental ideas
○   a lot of resource material and stimuli and time to experiment

II: *Deciding on course work*

Three points have become clear so far:

1   Most third-year classes have some 'non-composers'.
2   The methods, interests and musical abilities of the composers are often by now very different and diverse.
3   The composers need more flexibility in determining their method of working. Group work has become less appropriate for some of them.

How, then, do we devise a course of work which takes account of all of these needs?

For us the ideal solution has been to develop a project-based third-year course. This provides the class with a number of options, some of which are related to composing. It takes quite a lot of time to set up and its content will obviously depend upon the availability of resources. It might be, therefore, that for two or three years, especially if we are starting from scratch, the course will not be running perfectly, but it is possible to build it up in stages.

Let us look in detail at ways of devising projects for pupils like those we have introduced, i.e. those who want to continue composing. This is one of those situations where the teacher's own style of working, combined with knowledge of particular pupils, is going to be the most important factor in determining the nature of the course. Nevertheless, we have found it useful to have the following three categories in mind when planning the overall course to include the composing options:

1   composing assignments
2   integrated arts projects
3   integrated music projects

II: *Composing assignments*

It is not necessary for these to be directly related to any other work. As assignments they must be sufficiently flexible to be applicable to a number of different pupils (no teacher can be expected to design hundreds of individually tailored assignments every week), but we must be ready to respond to individual needs which become apparent once the assignments are under way. This is not as daunting as it sounds.

We need a good stock of source material for ideas, and this must be accessible to the pupils. For example:

o   Sets of work cards derived from suggestions in published books and adapted for particular pupils. (If the third-year pupils have had a comprehensive two-year composing course they should be able to cope with this method.)

o   Collections of literary or visual stimuli: paintings, poems, video tapes (silent films), advertisements with no sound

o   Aural resources: collections of tapes of varied styles of music to give inspiration/motivation for ideas of different kinds of music

The course work for composing consists of completing a number of topics either from these options or from their own ideas. We would expect the pupils to keep a record of their composing work, and the composing assessment sheet on page 114 suggests points we should want them to bear in mind.

Here are some examples of the kind of assignments we would prepare for those of our pupils who might choose this option.

Andrew

For pupils like Andrew, getting suitable material together is quite challenging as he has to work on his own some of the time. Because he has problems with reading, work cards are less suitable than tape recordings to guide him through ideas. For some of the suggested lessons we would record the information onto a cassette.

Cripps   *Popular Music in the Twentieth Century*, Assignment 7
Cain   *Keynote*, Chapter 2 'Making a melody'
Winters   *Sounds and Music*, Book 1 'Festivals'. Although this book is generally more suitable for first-years, some of the ideas are still appealing to Andrew. We've chosen this example for its good clear instructions.

Composing assessment sheet

Fill in as much of this as you can when you finish each project.
Keep these together in your file.

Name...

Title or type of composition...

Instruments/voices used..

Group/pair/single composition..

Who else did you work with?...

Where did the idea for this piece come from?..

Is there anything you would want to tell your listeners about your piece?

Is there any special reason for choosing the particular instruments/voices
for this piece?

Are there any comments you would like to make about the way that you
worked?

Did you have enough time to complete your piece?

Were you satisfied with it when it was finished? Any comments?

Did any other pupils/the teacher make useful comments about the piece
during the composition or at the end?

Did your final piece work out the way you thought it would?

Jane

Cain   *Keynote*, Chapter 11 'Chords' (composing variations)
Cripps *Popular Music in the Twentieth Century*, Assignment 37
These are both examples of the clear sets of step-by-step instructions which suit Jane best.

Peter

Cripps *Popular Music in the Twentieth Century*, Assignments 44–45
This is a good lesson for Peter because it expands his familiarity with chord sequences and gives him the opportunity to compose a pop song.

Lisa

Paynter and Aston   *Sound and Silence*, Projects 19B and 21B
The use of these two different scales (pentatonic and whole tone) satisfies Lisa's need for structures, but also gives her something new to work with. We would expect Lisa to be able to work straight from the book.

Matthew

Forster   *Music Lab*, 'Which note is which?' pages 34–37
The style of this book is particularly suitable to Matthew's way of working. These four pages contain a lot of ideas and information. Unlike Jane, who needs step-by-step instructions, Matthew responds to this kind of approach where the tasks are much more open-ended.

Thomas

Paynter and Aston   *Sound and Silence*,   Project 14B   'Exploring the piano (2)'
This quite sophisticated project is suitable for Thomas as a third-year as it goes well beyond the early exploratory stages with the piano. We would hope that he could assimilate some of the techniques from this project in future compositions.

Cain   *Keynote*, Chapter 8 'Semitones and whole tones'
This is a good lesson for making use of chromatic and whole tone scales. This assignment is good for consolidating Thomas's present skills.

Oliver

Vulliamy and Lee   *Pop, Rock and Ethnic Music in School*, Chapter 12,
          Projects 1, 2, 3 and 4
These projects are very clearly outlined for teachers but would need to be
adapted to work cards for pupils.

Forster *Music Lab*, page 51 'Pieces of music'
This would encourage Oliver to experiment on his instruments.

Paynter and Aston   *Sound and Silence*, Project 30B 'Major and minor
          modes' and Project 22B 'Notes, modes and rondos'
Cain   *Keynote*, Chapter 19 'Rondo form'
Between them these projects, and others like them, should help to
develop Oliver's understanding of the kind of music he can already play,
and encourage him to experiment outside these styles. There is a useful
appendix called 'Composers' Resource Bank' at the end of John
Howard's *Learning to Compose*. Some of Winter's projects in *Listen,
Compose, Perform* are suitable for more able third-year pupils.

II: *Integrated arts projects*

In these projects the third-year course is developed further
through work which incorporates other expressive arts: dance, drama,
mime, theatre, literature, fine arts and creative media studies. These are
all areas through which a project can develop if conditions for working in
this way are right. Many schools operate an integrated timetable for these
subjects where pupils are able to respond creatively through a variety of
media. If a project is stimulating enough and there is scope for incorporating work beyond the field of music, and if we feel capable and competent
to develop this, we should not feel prevented from doing so.

There are, perhaps, just two points to bear in mind here. First,
that we can cope with the directions in which the work is going and can
seek help and advice when we need it; and secondly, taking the year as a
whole, that our general aims for all these pupils will be fulfilled.

Some examples of books that music teachers might have which
contain good ideas for work in this area are as follows:

Ellis	*Out of Bounds*
Farmer	*Music in Practice*
Paynter and Paynter	*The Dance and the Drum*
Paynter and Aston	*Sound and Silence*

II: *Integrated music projects*

These are based on single musical ideas and include both composing and non-composing activities. This is a very manageable approach when there are a number of non-composers in the class because they can work alongside the composers. All participants can benefit from each other's work. As well as promoting lively group work, this approach gives pupils like Oliver the opportunity to work in some detail on all aspects of the musical topic. It can give Andrew a variety of things to do which hold his interest. It also provides the opportunity for them both to be involved in the same project.

Some examples of books which contain useful projects are as follows:

Cain	*Keynote*
Cripps	*Popular Music in the Twentieth Century*
Winters	*Sounds and Music* series
Bennett	*Enjoying Music*
McLeish and McLeish	*Oxford Topics in Music*

A combination of the above options should cater for the variety of pupils that we have in the third year. We particularly aim for more flexibility and divergence in our approach with this year, as well as offering a course which is demanding for our most musically capable pupils. In this way the pupils can use the skills they have developed in their first two years; and by the end of the third year some pupils will have begun to develop a degree of independence and autonomy in their composing work. Hopefully, through the structured work in all areas of their music curriculum for the whole of these first three years, all pupils will have benefited from a full and complete music course. Those who go on to do music in their fourth year will have a firm foundation for the composing element of their GCSE course and we hope that they will have begun to understand what it means to compose.

II: *Some pupils' comments on group work*

Composing my own music was quite good aspecially when we worked in groups. The hardest thing about composing my own music was trying to get the right texture. I don't really think we had any problems just that some people are fussy so we just tell them to shut up and get on with it. I would rather work in a group than by myself because when I'm with people I can discuss things with them. I can sometimes make my own ideas up and we use them in the group or sometimes their not very good so I don't say anything.

I don't really no if I could make my own music up I suppose I could but I'd rather have a partener.

The hardest part about composing I think is choosing the right instrument and rythm. The problems I came across was choosing the right notes.

I think working in groups is a good idea. You can share your ideas, and can work much faster. I like tunes that I can fit ~~tune~~ words to. So I can sing them in my mind and it helps me to remember the tune.

Working in groups is good because you can share ideas, which means you can composemusic faster. If you start talking you might get into a conversation and forget about your work.

We split up in to groups. In our group there is me,-SARAH HORNSBY, Joanne Blench, Lorraine Best, David Smith and Paul Smith. I was picked to be the captain of our group so my title was choosen. The title is 'The Fair Ground' and we decided on the instruments we each would use. We decided ~~that~~ ~~the~~ I Sarah would play the xylophone and Joanne would play the silver chime bars and Lorraine would play the black chime bars. Then I decided that David would play the drum and Paul would play the Indian bells and the maracas. After we had sorted that out I went round each one of our group and asked them to play a little tune on their instrument to get the feel of them and detect the rhythm. We then decided what instrument to enter first. Eventually we decided on the silver chime bars

119

played by Joanne. I had to help
Joanne get the right tune and I
showed her the way to bounce the
beater off the chime bars to make
it resond longer and soon she got
the hang of it. Next I thought David
should enter the drum so we could
have a beat all the way through the
piece of music and he soon too
got the hang of it. Next we entered
Indian Bells played by Paul. I showed
him how to play his part of the
music. At first he was a little difficult to handle but not so long after he
was great. He helped the rest of the
group and they all started to make
suggestions even if I ruled over
them sometimes they all had their
own oppinions of things which was
great. Next we entered Lorraine
with the black chime bars, she
made her own tune which I altered
a little bit. Next we entered Paul
with the maracas. He too made his
own tune with a little help from me.
We then entered the silver chime bars
again and repeated the tune. Last of
all I came in with the xylophone. I
thought of my own tune with help
from the others. We never got around
to fixing it all together because the
bell went but I know what I will
do. I will go through it altering anything I think needs it and ask all
the group their opinoins of the
work and give my own and that
will be the end of our piece of

music. Last of all I think every person in our group worked really hard at this piece of music and all showed equally, amounts of enthusiactly hard ship. They all were very cheerful people too work with and I'd like to work with them again.

I enjoyed working in pairs until you had a song composed then got a group together so that we could have some harmony in it

The most difficult part of composing is trying to find harmony and how to fit it in.

The hardest part of composing is chosing the instroments and organising the group. How played what. I lernt that you have to concentrate very hard or you will get know were.

If you composE on your own , you get some ideas but not a lot but if you are in a group you get all the ideas together and pick the best ones and it is fun as well. It is fun when you are in a group because you can experiment with different sounds, but some times if there is too many in the group you never get finished so the best way for me is about 4-5 in a group.

The advantages of working on your own are you dont fight which Ideas to put in. The disadvantages are that you don't have enough People to play the instroments.

I learned that composing isn't just writing rhyming words down but it's writing down feelings and frustrations and then singing them out.

I prefer to work on my own in music because when I work with others I just end up arguing with others and doing more work, then most of the others (sometimes) and I find it easier to concentrate when I am alone.

The most difficult part of composing is when I have to think about the basic formula to

build the song on
I did not have any bad
problems.

When you work in a
group you either don't
get a say in what should
go where or you do
more work than anyone
else the only advantage
that I can think of is
that when you are in
a group other people
are there to help when
you are stuck.
When you are on your
own you can concentrate
more.
I think we should learn
to compose on our
own if we choose
to because some people
prefer to work on their
own.
I think music should not
be wrote, but memorized.
Our most successful pei piece
was 'Snowflakes' it was a
very nice song.

last year in groups we compose 8 different tunes.

What we learnt from these compisitions was how to make different sounds and contrases fit together.

I prefer to write, music myself but have a little help with the lyrics and actual playing of the finished compisition.

I think the most difficult part of composing is getting different sounds to fit together. When there is more than two people in a group they tend to argue and carry on. It is good to work in groups so you have more than one idea. This year I think we should work by ourselves to find out what we come up with. I think we shoul write music down for future reference.

I think most of the m
I done was round about
the same this year

Composing is where you make up a peice of music.
In our peice we used the piano, xylophones
and a cymbal and indian bells.
We used these instruments to create an
affect of a good witch trying to over rule
a bad witch.
The hardest thing about composing is at the
begining when you try to find a good
affect to go with your title.
I think composing is good because I like
using different instruments.
I like working in groupes because you
can use more instruments in your peice.
Sometimes it is hard working in groups
because members might disagree with your
contribution to the group.
You can use your thoughts because you
can blend the thoughts together.

II: *A book selection*

Attwood, Tony *The Pop Songbooks*, Books 1, 2 and 3 (Oxford University Press, 1986)
Bennett, Roy *Enjoying Music*, Books 1, 2 and 3 and Workbooks 1, 2 and 3 (Longman, 1977–81)
Chatterley, Albert *The Music Club Book of Improvisation Projects* (Galliard, 1978)
Cain, Tim *Keynote* (Cambridge University Press, 1988)
Cripps, Colin *Popular Music in the Twentieth Century*, Cambridge Assignments in Music series, edited by Roy Bennett and Michael Burnett (Cambridge University Press, 1988)
Dennis, Brian *Projects in Sound* (Universal Edition, 1975)
Ellis, Phil *Out of Bounds* (Oxford University Press, 1987)
Farmer, Paul (ed.) *Longman Music Topics* (Longman, 1979)
Farmer, Paul (ed.) *Music in Practice* (Oxford University Press, 1984)
Forster, John *Music Lab* (Universal Edition, 1983)
Howard, John *Learning to Compose* (Cambridge University Press, 1989)
McLeish, Kenneth and McLeish, Valerie (eds.) *Oxford Topics in Music* series (Oxford University Press, 1982)
Paynter, John *Hear and Now: an introduction to modern music in schools* (Universal Edition, 1972)
Paynter, John *Sound Tracks* series (Cambridge University Press, 1978)
Paynter, John and Aston, Peter *Sound and Silence: Classroom Projects in Creative Music* (Cambridge University Press, 1970)
Paynter, John and Paynter, Elizabeth *The Dance and the Drum* (Universal Edition, 1974)
Tillman, June *Exploring Sound: creative musical projects for teachers* (Galliard, 1976)
Vulliamy, Graham and Lee, Ed *Pop, Rock and Ethnic Music in School*, Resources of Music series, General editor John Paynter (Cambridge University Press, 1982)
Winters, Geoffrey *Sounds and Music*, Books 1, 2 and 3 (Longman, 1978–80)
Winters, Geoffrey *Listen, Compose, Perform* (Longman, 1986)

II: *General reference*

Brandes, D. and Phillips, H. *Gamesters' Handbook* (Hutchinson Educational, 1986)
Department of Education and Science *Music from 5 to 16*, Curriculum Matters 4 (HMSO, 1985)
Paynter, John *Music in the Secondary School Curriculum* (Cambridge University Press, 1982)
Ross, Malcolm *The Creative Arts* (Heinemann, 1978)
Salaman, William *Living School Music* (Cambridge University Press, 1983)